CW00591619

A BOLT OF
WHITE CLOTH

ALSO BY LEON ROOKE

Sing Me No Love Songs
I'll Say You No Prayers

Shakespeare's Dog

The Birth Control King
of the Upper Volta

Death Suite

Fat Woman

The Magician in Love

Cry Evil

The Broad Back of the Angel

The Love Parlour

Vault

Last One Home
Sleeps in the Yellow Bed

AUTHOR OF SHAKESPEARE'S DOG

LEON ROOKE

A BOLT OF WHITE CLOTH

THE ECCO PRESS/NEW YORK

Copyright © 1984 by Leon Rooke
All rights reserved
No part of this book may be reproduced or
transmitted by any means, electronic or mechanical,
including photography, recording, or any
information or retrieval system, without
permission in writing from the publisher.

FIRST PUBLISHED BY ECCO PRESS IN 1985
18 West 30th Street, New York, New York 10001

Published in Canada by
Stoddard Publishing,
A division of General Publishing Co. Limited

Library of Congress Cataloguing in Publication Data

Rooke, Leon.
A bolt of white cloth.

Contents: A bolt of white cloth — The only
daughter — Why the heathens are no more — (etc.)

I. Title.

PS3568.06B6   1984   813'.54   84–18868
ISBN 0-88001-078-9

Cover design by Brant Cowie / Artplus Ltd.

Cover Painting: *Pandora's Box* by Jane Zednik,
oil on canvas, 30" x 30", 1982.

Printed and bound in Canada

Contents

A Bolt of White Cloth

A MAN CAME BY our road carrying an enormous bolt of white cloth on his back. Said he was from the East. Said whoever partook of this cloth would come to know true happiness. Innocence without heartbreak, he said, if that person proved worthy. My wife fingered his cloth, having in mind something for new curtains. It was good quality, she said. Beautifully woven, of a fine, light texture, and you certainly couldn't argue with the color.

"How much is it?" she asked.

"Before I tell you that," the man said, "you must tell me truthfully if you've ever suffered."

"Oh, I've suffered," she said. "I've known suffering of some description every day of my natural life."

I was standing over by the toolshed, with a big smile. My wife is a real joker, who likes nothing better than pulling a person's leg. She's known hardships, this and that upheaval, but nothing I would call down-and-out suffering. Mind you, I don't speak for her. I wouldn't pretend to speak for another person.

This man with the bolt of cloth, however, he clearly had no sense of my wife's brand of humor. She didn't get an itch of a smile out of him. He kept the cloth neatly balanced on his shoulder, wincing a little from the weight and from however far he'd had to carry it, staring hard and straight at my wife the whole time she fooled with him, as if he hoped to peer clear through to her soul. His eyes were dark and brooding and hollowed out some. He was like no person either my wife or me had ever seen before.

"Yes," he said, "but suffering of what kind?"

"Worse than I hope forever to carry, I'll tell you that," my wife said. "But why are you asking me these questions? I like your cloth and if the price is right I mean to buy it."

"You can only buy my cloth with love," he said.

We began right then to understand that he was some kind of oddity. He was not like anybody we'd ever seen and he didn't come from around here. He'd come from a place we'd never heard of, and if that was the East, or wherever, then he was welcome to it.

"Love?" she said. "Love? There's *love* and there's *love*, mister. What kind are you talking about?" She hitched a head my way, rolling her eyes, as if to indicate that if it was *passionate* love he was talking about then he'd first have to do something with me. He'd have to get me off my simmer and onto full boil. That's what she was telling him, with this mischief in her eyes.

I put down my pitchfork about here, and strolled nearer. I liked seeing my wife dealing with difficult situations. I didn't want to miss anything. My life with that woman has been packed with the unusual. Unusual circumstances, she calls them. Any time she's ever gone out anywhere without me, whether for a day or an hour or for five minutes, she's come back with whopping good stories about what she's seen and heard and what's happened to her. She's come back with reports on these unusual circumstances, these little adventures in which so many people have done so many extraordinary things or behaved in such fabulous or foolish ways. So what was rare this time, I thought, was that it had come visiting. She hadn't had to go out and find it.

"Hold these," my wife told me. And she put this washtub of

clothes in my hands, and went back to hanging wet pieces on the line, which is what she'd been doing when this man with the bolt of cloth ventured up into our yard.

"Love," she told him. "You tell me what kind I need, if I'm to buy that cloth. I got good ears and I'm listening."

The man watched her stick clothespins in her mouth, slap out a good wide sheet, and string it up. He watched her hang two of these, plus a mess of towels, and get her mouth full again before he spoke. He looked about the unhappiest I've ever seen any man look. He didn't have any joy in him. I wondered why he didn't put down that heavy bolt of cloth, and why he didn't step around into a spot of shade. The sun was lick-killing bright in that yard. I was worried he'd faint.

"The ordinary kind," he said. "Your ordinary kind of love will buy this cloth."

My wife flapped her wash and laughed. He was really tickling her. She was having herself a wonderful time.

"What's ordinary?" she said. "I've never known no *ordinary* love."

He jumped right in. He got excited just for a second.

"The kind such as might exist between the closest friends," he said. "The kind such as might exist between a man and his wife or between parents and children or for that matter the love a boy might have for his dog. That kind of love."

"I've got that," she said. "I've had all three. Last year this time I had me a fourth, but it got run over. Up on the road there, by the tall trees, by a man in a car who didn't even stop."

"That would have been your cat," he said. "I don't know much about cats."

I put down the washtub. My wife let her arms drop. We looked at him, wondering how he knew about that cat. Then I laughed, for I figured someone down the road must have told him of my wife's mourning over that cat. She'd dug it a grave under the grapevine and said sweet words over it. She sorely missed that cat.

"What's wrong with loving cats?" she asked him. "Or beasts of the fields? I'm surprised at you."

The man shifted his burden and worked one shoe into the ground. He stared off at the horizon. He looked like he knew he'd said something he shouldn't.

She pushed me out of the way. She wanted to get nearer to him. She had something more to say.

"Now listen to me," she said. "I've loved lots of things in my life. Lots and lots. *Him!*" she said (pointing at me), *"it"* (pointing to our house), *"them!"* (pointing to the flower beds), *"that!"* (pointing to the sky), *"those"* (pointing to the woods), *"this"* (pointing to the ground) — "practically *everything!* There isn't any of it I've hated, and not much I've been indifferent to. Including cats. So put that in your pipe and smoke it."

Then swooping up her arms and laughing hard, making it plain she bore no grudge but wasn't just fooling.

Funny thing was, hearing her say it, I felt the same way. *It, them, that, those* — they were all beautiful. I couldn't deny it was love I was feeling.

The man with the cloth had turned each way she'd pointed. He'd staggered a time or two but he'd kept up. In fact, it struck me that he'd got a little ahead of her. That he knew where her arm was next going. Some trickle of pleasure was showing in his face. And something else was happening, something I'd never seen. He had his face lifted up to this burning sun. It was big and orange, that sun, and scorching-hot, but he was staring smack into it. He wasn't blinking or squinting. His eyes were wide open.

Madness or miracle, I couldn't tell which.

He strode over to a parcel of good grass.

"I believe you mean it," he said. "How much could you use?"

He placed the bolt of white cloth down on the grass and pulled out shiny scissors from his back pocket.

"I bet he's blind," I whispered to my wife. "I bet he's got false eyes."

My wife shushed me. She wasn't listening. She had her excitement hat on; her *unusual circumstances* look. He was offering free cloth for love, ordinary love, and she figured she'd go along with the gag.

How much?

"Oh," she said, "maybe eight yards. Maybe ten. It depends on how many windows I end up doing, plus what hang I want, plus the pleating I'm after."

"You mean to make these curtains yourself?" he asked. He was already down on his knees, smoothing the bolt. Getting set to roll it out.

"Why, sure," she said. "I don't know who else would do it for me. I don't know who else I would ask."

He nodded soberly, not thinking about it. "That's so," he said casually. "Mend your own fences first." He was perspiring in the sun, and disheveled, as though he'd been on the road a long time. His shoes had big holes in them and you could see the blistered soles of his feet, but he had an air of exhilaration now. His hair fell down over his eyes and he shoved the dark locks back. I got the impression that some days he went a long time between customers; that he didn't find cause to give away this cloth every day.

He got a fair bit unrolled. It certainly did look like prime goods, once you saw it spread out on the grass in that long expanse.

"It's so pretty!" My wife said. "Heaven help me, but I think it is *prettier* than grass!"

"It's pretty, all right," he said. "It's a wing-dinger. Just tell me when to stop," he said. "Just shout yoo-hoo."

"Hold up a minute," she said. "I don't want to get greedy. I don't want you rolling off more than we can afford."

"You can afford it," he said.

He kept unrolling. He was up past the well house by now,

whipping it off fast, though the bolt didn't appear to be getting any smaller. My wife had both hands up over her mouth. Half of her wanted to run into the house and get her purse so she could pay; the other half wanted to stay and watch this man unfurl his beautiful cloth. She whipped around to me, all agitated.

"I believe he means it," she said. "He means us to have this cloth. What do I do?"

I shook my head. This was her territory. It was the kind of adventure constant to her nature and necessary to her well-being.

"Honey," I said, "you deal with it."

The sun was bright over everything. It was whipping-hot. There wasn't much wind but I could hear the clothes flapping on the line. A woodpecker had himself a pole somewhere and I could hear him pecking. The sky was wavy blue. The trees seemed to be swaying.

He was up by the front porch now, still unrolling. It surprised us both that he could move so fast.

"Yoo-hoo," my wife said. It was no more than a peep, the sound you might make if a butterfly lands on your hand.

"Wait," he said. "One thing. One question I meant to ask. All this talk of love, your *it*, your *those* and *them*, it slipped my mind."

"Let's hear it," my wife said. "Ask away." It seemed to me that she spoke out of a trance. That she was as dazzled as I was.

"You two got no children," he said. "Why is that? You're out here on this nice farm, and no children to your name. Why is that?"

We hadn't expected this query from him. It did something to the light in the yard and how we saw it. It was as if some giant dark bird had fluttered between us and the sun. Without knowing it, we sidled closer to each other. We fumbled for the other's hand. We stared off every which way. No one on our road had asked that question in a long, long time; they hadn't asked it in some years.

"We're not able," we said. Both of us spoke at the same time. It seemed to me that it was my wife's voice which carried; mine was some place down in my chest, and dropping, as if it meant to crawl on the ground.

"We're not able," we said. That time it came out pure, without any grief to bind it. It came out the way we long ago learned how to say it.

"Oh," he said. "I see." He mumbled something else. He kicked the ground and took a little walk back and forth. He seemed angry, though not at us. "Wouldn't you know it?" he said. "Wouldn't you know it?"

He swore a time or two. He kicked the ground. He surely didn't like it.

"We're over that now," my wife said. "We're past that caring."

"I bet you are," he said. "You're past that little misfortune."

He took to unrolling his bolt again, working with his back to the sun. Down on his knees, scrambling, smoothing the material. Sweating and huffing. He was past the front porch now, and still going, getting on toward that edge where the high weeds grew.

"About here, do you think?" he asked.

He'd rolled off about fifty yards.

My wife and I slowly shook our heads, not knowing what to think.

"Say the word," he told us. "I can give you more if more is what you want."

"I'd say you were giving us too much," my wife said. "I'd say we don't need nearly that much."

"Never mind that," he said. "I'm feeling generous today."

He nudged the cloth with his fingers and rolled off a few yards more. He would have gone on unwinding his cloth had the weeds not stopped him. He stood and looked back over the great length he had unwound.

"Looks like a long white road, don't it?" he said. "You could walk that road and your feet never get dirty."

My wife clenched my hand; it was what we'd both been thinking.

SnipSnipSnip. He began snipping. His scissors raced over the material. *SnipSnipSnip.* The cloth was sheared clear and clean of his bolt, yet it seemed to me the size of that bolt hadn't lessened any. My wife saw it too.

"He's got cloth for all eternity," she said. "He could unroll that cloth till doomsday."

The man laughed. We were whispering this, but way up by the weeds he heard us. "There's doom and there's doom," he said. "*Which* doomsday?"

I had the notion he'd gone through more than one. That he knew the picture from both sides.

"It *is* smart as grass," he said. "Smarter. It never needs watering." He chuckled at that, spinning both arms. Dancing a little. "You could make *nighties* out of this," he said. "New bedsheets. Transform your whole bedroom."

My wife made a face. She wasn't too pleased, talking *nighties* with another man.

Innocence without heartbreak, I thought. That's what we're coming to.

He nicely rolled up the cloth he'd sheared off and presented it to my wife. "I hope you like it," he said. "No complaints yet. Maybe you can make yourself a nice dress as well. Maybe two or three. Make him some shirts. I think you'll find there's plenty here."

"Goodness, it's light," she said.

"Not if you've been carrying it long as I have," he said. He pulled a blue bandanna from his pocket and wiped his face and neck. He ran his hand through his hair and slicked it back. He looked up at the sky. His dark eyes seemed to have cleared up some. They looked less broody now. "Gets hot," he said, "working in this sun. But a nice day. I'm glad I found you folks home."

"Oh, we're most always home," my wife said.

I had to laugh at that. My wife almost never *is* home. She's forever gallivanting over the countryside, checking up on this person and that, taking them her soups and jams and breads.

"We're homebodies, us two."

She kept fingering the cloth and sighing over it. She held it up against her cheek and with her eyes closed rested herself on it. The man hoisted his own bolt back on his shoulder; he seemed ready to be going. I looked at my wife's closed lids, at the soft look she had.

I got trembly, fearful of what might happen if that cloth didn't work out.

"Now look," I said to him, "what's wrong with this cloth? Is it going to rot inside a week? Tomorrow is some *other* stranger going to knock on our door saying we owe him a hundred or five hundred dollars for this cloth? Mister, I don't understand you," I said.

He hadn't bothered with me before; now he looked me dead in the eye. "I can't help being a stranger," he said. "If you never set eyes on me before, I guess that's what I would have to be. Don't you like strangers? Don't you trust them?"

My wife jumped in. Her face was fiery, like she thought I had wounded him. "We like strangers just fine," she said. "We've helped out many a-one. No, I can't say our door has ever been closed to whoever it is comes by. Strangers can sit in our kitchen just the same as our friends."

He smiled at her but kept his stern look for me. "As to your questions," he said, "You're worried about the golden goose, I can see that. Fair enough. No, your cloth will not rot. It will not shred, fade, or tear. Nor will it ever need cleaning, either. This cloth requires no upkeep whatsoever. Though a sound heart helps. A sweet disposition, too. Innocence without heartbreak, as I told you. And your wife, if it's her making the curtains or making herself a dress, she will find it to be an amazingly easy cloth to work with. It will practically do the job itself. No, I don't believe you will ever find you have any reason to complain of the quality of that cloth."

My wife had it up to her face again. She had her face sunk in it.

"Goodness," she said, "it's *soft*! It smells so fresh. It's like someone singing a song to me."

The man laughed. "It *is* soft," he said. "But it can't sing a note, or has never been known to."

It was my wife singing. She had this little hum under the breath.

"This is the most wonderful cloth in the world," she said.

He nodded. "I can't argue with you on that score," he said. Then he turned again to me. "I believe your wife is satisfied," he said. "But if you have any doubts, if you're worried someone is going to knock on your door tomorrow asking you for a hundred or five hundred dollars, I suppose I could write you up a guarantee. I could give you a PAID IN FULL."

He was making me feel ashamed of myself. They both were. "No, no," I said, "if she's satisfied then I am. And I can see she's tickled pink. No, I beg your pardon. I meant no offense."

"No offense taken," he said.

But his eyes clouded a token. He gazed off at our road and up along the stand of trees and his eyes kept roaming until they snagged the sun. He kept his eyes there, unblinking, open, staring at the sun. I could see the red orbs reflected in his eyes.

"There is one thing," he said.

I caught my breath and felt my wife catch hers. The hitch? A hitch, after all? Coming so late?

We waited.

He shuffled his feet. He brought out his bandanna and wiped his face again. He stared at the ground.

"Should you ever stop loving," he said, "you shall lose this cloth and all else. You shall wake up one morning and it and all else will no longer be where you left it. It will all be gone and you will not know where you are. You will not know what to do with yourself. You will wish you'd never been born."

My wife's eyes went saucer-size.

He had us in some kind of spell.

Hocus-pocus, I thought. He is telling us some kind of hocus-pocus. Yet I felt my skin shudder; I felt the goose bumps rise.

"That's it?" my wife said. "That's the only catch?"

He shrugged. "That's it," he said. "Not much, is it? Not a whisper of menace for a pair such as yourselves."

My wife's eyes were gauzed over; there was a wetness in them.

"Hold on," she said. "Don't you be leaving yet. Hold this, honey."

She put the cloth in my arms. Then she hastened over to the well, pitched the bucket down, and drew it up running over with fresh water.

"Here," she said, coming back with a good dipperful. "Here's a nice drink of cool water. You need it on a day like this."

The man drank. He held the dipper in both hands, with the tips of his fingers, and drained the dipper dry, then wiped his chin with the back of a hand.

"I did indeed," he said. "That's very tasty water. I thank you."

"That's good water," she said. "That well has been here lo a hundred years. You could stay on for supper," she said. "It's getting on toward that time and I have a fine stew on the stove, with plenty to spare."

"That's kind of you," he said back, "and I'm grateful. But I'd best pass on up your road while there's still daylight left, and see who else might have need of this cloth."

My wife is not normally a demonstrative woman, not in public. Certainly not with strangers. You could have knocked me over with a feather when she up and kissed him full on the mouth, with a nice hug to boot.

"There's payment," she said, "if our money's no good."

He blushed, trying to hide his pleasure. It seemed to me she had him wrapped around her little finger...or the other way around.

"You kiss like a woman," he said. "Like one who knows what kissing is for, and can't hardly stop herself."

It was my wife's turn to blush.

I took hold of her hand and held her down to grass, because it seemed to me another kiss or two and she'd fly right away with him.

He walked across the yard and up by the well house, leaving by the same route he had come. Heading for the road. At the turn, he spun around and waved.

"You could try the Hopkins place!" my wife called. "There's a fat woman down that road got a sea of troubles. She could surely use some of that cloth."

He smiled and again waved. Then we saw his head and his bolt of white cloth bobbing along the weeds as he took the dips and rises in the road. Then he went on out of sight.

"There's that man with some horses down that road!" my wife called. "You be careful of him!"

It seemed we heard some sound come back, but whether it was his we couldn't say.

My wife and I stood a long time in the yard, me holding the dipper and watching her, while she held her own bolt of cloth in her arms, staring off to where he'd last been.

Then she sighed dreamily and went inside.

I went on down to the barn and looked after the animals. Getting my feeding done. I talked a spell to them. Talking to animals is soothing to me, and they like it too. They pretend to stare at the walls or the floor as they're munching their feed down, but I know they listen to me. We had us an *unusual circumstances* chat. "That man with the cloth," I said. "Maybe you can tell me what you make of him."

Thirty minutes later I heard my wife excitedly calling me. She was standing out on the back doorstep, with this incredulous look.

"I've finished," she said. "I've finished the windows. *Nine* windows. It beats me how."

I started up to the house. Her voice was all shaky. Her face flushed, flinging her arms about. Then she got this new look on.

"Wait!" she said. "Stay there! Give me ten minutes!"

And she flung herself back inside, banging the door. I laughed. It always gave me a kick how she ordered me around.

I got the milk pail down under the cow. Before I'd touched and drained all four teats she was calling again.

"Come look, come look, oh come look!"

She was standing in the open doorway, with the kitchen to her back. Behind her, through the windows, I could see the streak of a red sunset and how it lit up the swing of trees. But I wasn't looking there. I was looking at her. Looking and swallowing hard and trying to remember how a body produced human speech. I had never thought of white as a color she could wear. White, it pales her some. It leaves her undefined and washes out what parts I like best. But she looked beautiful now. In her new dress she struck me down to my bootstraps. She made my chest break.

"Do you like it?" she said.

I went running up to her. I was up against her, hugging her and lifting her before she'd even had a chance to get set. I'd never held on so tightly or been so tightly held back.

Truth is, it was the strangest thing. Like we were both so innocent we hadn't yet shot up out of new ground.

"Come see the curtains," she whispered. "Come see the new sheets. Come see what else I've made. You'll see it all. You'll see how our home has been transformed."

I crept inside. There was something holy about it. About it and about us and about those rooms and the whole wide world. Something radiant. Like you had to put your foot down easy and hold it down or you'd float on up.

"That's it," she said. "That's how I feel too."

That night in bed, trying to figure it out, we wondered how Ella Mae down the road had done. How the people all along our road had made out.

"No worry," my wife said. "He'll have found a bonanza

around here. There's heaps of decent people in this neck of the woods."

"Wonder where he is now?" we said.

"Wonder where he goes next?"

"Where he gets that cloth?"

"Who he *is*?"

We couldn't get to sleep, wondering about that.

The Only Daughter

THE LANE UPON which the child walked was long and straight, with high red-dirt walls to either side, which sometimes she could see above and other times could not. It was more trench than road, wide enough perhaps for three people to walk abreast, perhaps wide enough for a wagon. Yes, for a wagon, for she could see in the slippery mud where one had come and gone, though not when. The walls were eroded by rain and where boulders were packed into the dirt scraggly bushes, leafless now, made vain attempts at renewal. She walked mostly in the lane's middle, trying to avoid the collected puddles, since her shoes were new, or newish, and she yet took some pride in them. Suitcases half her own height hung from each arm. She had started the day with a ribbon through her hair, tied at the top in a bow, but at some point several miles back the ribbon had come loose and now lay unmissed in the mud. She wore, in addition to the shoes and a thin cotton dress, a black coat that flopped unevenly around her heels. A circle of mud, steadily expanding, caked the hem and seemed to pull the coat farther from her shoulders. From time to time, fretfully, she yanked it back. A single large button secured the coat; the button was ever traveling up to her throat; her heels were ever stepping onto the hem. The coat draped loosely on her, an adult's coat, inherited with something of that other person's shape still intact. The sleeves were twice folded at each wrist that her hands might be clear. It had had a belt once; she wished she had it now.

From time to time she paused and placed the suitcases on dry earth or on stumps, on weedy patches in the lane, and shook her arms until feeling returned to them.

She had been walking this lane since first light; she had traversed it for a portion of yesterday. Now the sun, although it brought no warmth, was directly overhead. It moved when she moved, and at what pace she moved, and stopped when she stopped. But she did not look often at the sun or sky; she kept her sight on the road, on her feet, for the lane was strewn with rock and brush, with brown puddles of varying size, with massive boulders that cropped up from floor and wall. Occasionally, where the land was flat, the woods encroached until the land all but disappeared. She went, at such times, the way the wheel tracks went, passing under pine and cedar, under hemlock and droopy locust, under willow and numerous other dusty, unswaying trees. Where red dirt receded, clumps of wild grass took over, competing with moss and clover, and here she took longer rests. With leaves and sticks she wiped new layers of mud from her shoes. Her feet were wet and cold, but she was accustomed to this and gave thought to it only when pebbles worked inside her shoes. She wore a grown woman's nylon stockings, which bunched at her ankles. Originally these had been retained by rubber bands just above her knees, but the bands, rotted already, had broken countless times and no longer held. One she sometimes chewed in her mouth, trudging along now at a diminishing pace.

Rests were more frequent now. Her shoulders ached. Her legs ached, and her arms and hands worst of all, though her feet ached too. Her shoes were too tight. The man at the store had told her they would loosen, but they hadn't. This morning they'd been stiff and hard, though still wet, and she'd opened a heel blister, getting them on. She'd bitten her lip and tears had come, but she'd kept them on. She was too cold to feel much

anyhow. Her hands were blistered too. They were swollen
some. The suitcase handles were sharp, like little razors. She'd
tried wrapping leaves about the handles but they'd shredded in
a minute. They'd been slippery too. Green stuff had got into
her cuts and stung. Maybe it was her hands that hurt the most.
She'd thought it was her hands, but she'd carried the cases a
few feet and the ache had hit her shoulders again. She was
hungry, but she wasn't going to think about that. The shoulder
ache was worse. Pins and needles stabbed down from her neck;
her neck was stiff. A stiff neck was nothing though. She could
put up with a stiff neck. The shoulder ache made her groan; it
made her grit her teeth. But after a while she'd decided it was
her arms that hurt more, the bones stretched near to bursting.
Nothing could hurt more than that. But she'd halt and put
down the cases and dangle her arms and shake that pain away.
She couldn't shake out the shoulder ache; shoulder was worse.
She was hungry, but she wasn't going to think about that. Heck
with that. What was bad was the button, which kept crawling
up, gnawing a hole at her throat, always in the same spot.
Maybe that was worse. Like somebody digging at it with an ice
pick or pinching that same spot over and over. This was the
most maddening somehow, because such a little thing. You
wouldn't believe a smooth button could be so sharp. The same
place over and over, her skin raw. Like her heels. Her heels
were bloody. These stockings were ruined. Well she didn't
mind that; she had plenty more. Maybe a dozen pair. She had a
hat too, but you didn't need a hat out here. A hat would be silly
out here. Mud was on her coat, but she couldn't help that. Mud
was nothing, you could wash out that. She hoped you could.
This dress she had on, you could sure wash that. She'd done so
herself, and ironed it too, not three days ago. Not that a person
would know it now. It was her shoes she most cared about.
They were pretty shoes. If she ruined them that would be her
bad luck because she had no other pair. But how could you ruin
cowhide? Cows got wet, they didn't ruin; no reason these

would either. She was hungry, but she wasn't going to think about that. Thinking about it only made matters worse. Last night she'd thought about it anyway, but only for a little while. Then she'd slept and thought about her aches. About which was worse. It was awful, whichever way you thought, but she wasn't going to cry about it any more than she was going to sit down in this lane and quit. She didn't mean to walk this road forever; aches would mend, cuts and blisters heal. She'd been tired before, tired a thousand times. Hungry too. But she'd got over it. She would this time too. So she bit her lip and let her eyes stay wet as they wanted to; she labored on. She'd be there pretty soon. This lane wasn't no endless highway going nowhere. She knew where it was going. Her instructions had been clear on that score. *Git out fast. Go to him. This is where he lives.*

Whenever she stopped now she would lay back if that were possible, and draw the big coat tight about herself, and close her eyes. She would doze. But always, after a minute or two she would bolt up as if from fright, and dig both hands into her coat pockets. The left pocket contained an unopened package of Luden's Wild Cherry cough drops, and five or six black hairpins when these did not happen to be in her hair. In the right pocket was a small leather change purse, much scarred. She would open it and empty it in her lap and count her money. Her fear was that she would lose this or that it somehow might be stolen. She feared pickpockets even here on this solitary lane, for long ago, in another place, her mother had screamed and yelled and cried because a pickpocket had got her money. She remembered that. She remembered her mother's alarm as she cried, "How can we live? Tell me how we can manage now!" She remembered her mother's alarm, and her own, but not how they had managed. She had noticed no difference in how they got along. They had moved, she remembered that. Her mother had been absent much of the time. This was because of the pickpocket. She knew that.

She had in her possession two quarters, three dimes, a nickel, and four pennies. Yesterday she had had more but the man on the bus had taken the dollar bill. He had taken the half-dollar too, and had seemed to want to take more, but she had bitten her lip, watching his every move, and thirty-nine cents had been miraculously returned to her palm. "How I know you're not cheatin' me?" she said. "How I know how much this bus trip is?" "You don't," he said. He'd had a cigarette dangling from his lips the whole time, and scabs on his hand. He'd had black hairs in his nose. "You don't. No, you don't. You don't know nothin', I expect." She'd not risen to this taunt. She'd kept her palm open, stretched out to him. "You want me to kiss it?" he said. "Maybe you want a glob of my spit?" She'd yanked her hand back, since it seemed no more change was forthcoming. She'd put the coins in her purse and the purse in her coat pocket, and staggered down the aisle with her two suitcases. She'd put the cases on a seat at the back where there was a big round hump in the floor. For resting your feet, she supposed. She climbed over them and sat at the window, which wouldn't open. "You see them racks?" he said. "Them racks is for the suitcases. Ain't you never traveled before?" He stood over her, his cigarette dangling, squinting at her. She'd thrown her body over the suitcases. "I ain't putting them nowhere," she said. "I ain't having my property stole."

He'd gone.

She talked to no one during the journey. The bus was nearly empty. A boy hardly out of diapers sat up front, making faces at her. She gave him her black look and kept her lips sewed tight. He came back once and said, "This ain't your bus. I never seen you on this bus before." When he went back to his seat his mother slapped him. She ought to have. She ought to have smacked him a dozen times. She curled up, making a careful, secret study of each inch of the interior. Cold wind came through the window. The tires whined. The seats were hard and squared off at the back where there was a rod you could lean your head against. The bus had a flat roof with rounded edges. The floor was nothing but tin. The seats weren't yellow though, like the dinette she and her mother used to have. The terrain outside was mostly a blur, and she told herself it wasn't worth looking at. The window was smeary anyhow.

It wasn't worth a bit what she'd paid.

In the afternoon, and repeatedly after that, she moved up the aisle to remind the man with the cigarette where she wanted to get off and to wonder aloud if he hadn't passed it already.

"Nobody told me it was this far," she said.

"That's right," he said. "You're abducted. This here is John Dillinger at the wheel."

"I don't care who you are. You better stop at that crossroads I told you about."

"It ain't no crossroads," he said. "It ain't hardly nothing. Just a scratch in the woods, that's all it is."

"Says you," she said.

"This here bus is heated," he told her. "Supposing you take off that there hot coat and try to relax yourself." She held her hand clenched over the purse in her pocket while she talked to him. She had no faith in him. He was one of them smart talkers, those her mother said you had to look out for. He looked to her like an out-and-out damn fool, with his stubbly growth of beard, with his scabs and dangling cigarette and his eyes squinted up so tight it surprised her he could see the road.

"Who you visiting?" he asked, but she locked her lips and veered back to her seat.

If he didn't stop where he was supposed to she didn't know what she'd do. She wondered what a body was supposed to do when it had to go to the bathroom. The boy up front got smacked again.

"It's going to rain," somebody said.

Somebody was always saying that. They got their brains out of a marble jug.

The man nearest her was eating a white apple. She'd never

seen no white apple before. It almost made her puke to watch him eat it. But she watched every bite he took, and when he had gnawed it down to seeds and core she saw him drop it on the floor. She wouldn't eat no white apple no matter how hungry she got. She wouldn't eat no turnips either, or spinach, or innards of any kind. She wouldn't eat no fatback either.

She had her cough drops, but she was saving them.

She gnawed her nails and kept her vigil; she didn't know when it was she fell asleep.

Near dark, the bus driver pulled to the side of the road. It was the bumps, and gravel hitting the underside, that woke her. "Somebody meeting you, I hope," he said. "I don't take no responsibility. This here bus line don't take none. Strange things go on in them woods. Wild animals, too. Naw sir, you wouldn't find me getting off at no godforsaken place like this. Not at nighttime no how."

This angered her. It angered her because his saying it scared her and because she knew he saw it.

"I don't see no crossroads," she said.

He offered to help with her suitcases, but she held tightly to them. The boy who'd made faces was asleep with his mouth open. He had a booger hanging from his nose and snot smeared across his cheek. The woman beside him was smoking, staring in a dull way at nothing. She didn't have no nice hose like her mother had worn. She didn't wear no rouge or lipstick either.

It was a real dumb load on that bus.

She followed the driver to the front of the bus. He put a foot on the bumper and leaned his elbow on his knee. His shirt was bunched up, and she could see his ugly naked skin. The air the bus lights shot through was smoky. It did little cartwheels in the beams. "There she is," he said, meaning the lane.

But she didn't see it.

"There ain't nothing," she said. "You've let me off at the wrong place." She wanted her money back, but didn't say it. He was still pointing. "It's there," he said. "You can call it a crossroads till gold comes out your behind, but your calling it so ain't going to change it none. It's that little lane you see yonder by the stump. It ain't hardly more than a red-dirt path and you can beat my rear end till doomsday and I'd still stay ignorant of where it goes. There was a house there once, or a store. I never seen no traffic come up out of that lane. I never had nobody go down it before. Far as I know there ain't a soul lives down that lane. Maybe a few squirrels and rabbits, maybe snakes, if they's got souls. I hope you come for a long visit cause you going to be in no shape to leave if ever you get where you're going. Be solid night soon. Looks to me like you took the wrong time to pay a call. But that's the road you ask for. That's Spider's Lane. You ask me, you're going to wish you'd stayed where you was."

He was a big blabbermouth. She would have told him so, but he was wrestling the suitcases from her. He tugged them from her hands and crossed the highway and plonked them down on the other side. She saw the lane now. Vines grew over it at the mouth. She still didn't see no stump.

"There you go," he said. "Service with a smile. I come by first thing in the morning, you want to go back, but you got to wave me down. Ticket cost the same, coming or going."

She picked up her cases and started off.

"You're uppity," he said, pitching his live cigarette into the ditch. "But I don't hold it against you. I reckon you never had no one to show you how to behave."

She called him a son of a bitch, with her teeth together and her eyes slitted, just the way her mother would have.

He sauntered back to his driver's seat. Two or three faces were at the greasy windows, mutely studying her. She heard the gears grind. Groaning, its twin beams slicing the dark, the bus moved on and after interminable seconds disappeared around the curve, its four blinkers still flashing.

She didn't believe this was the right place. Crossroads was what she'd been told to head down. But the sign, rotted where it entered the ground and thrust back into the bushes, had the right words on it, splashed on in a faded paint. *"Spider's Lane. You go down Spider's Lane till you're about to drop. When you've dropped I guess you'll be near enough."*

"But I don't want to go."

" 'Want' ain't got britches no more she can wear. 'Want' is dropped dead. I can't look out for you no more. 'Looking out' has finally got the best of me. You go."

"Yes'm."

"Are you going?"

"Yes'm."

"Then pull the covers up and let me sleep. Tuck me in."

"Yes'm."

She'd spent the night on pine straw in a hollow about a hundred feet off the road, camouflaging herself under broken branches, the coat pulled up over her head, the money purse in a fist up under her chin. She chewed on bitter pine bark and once or twice swallowed some. Her stomach churned. It was like someone inside trying to talk to her, refusing to shut up.

"I can't let you sleep with me. You'd kick. Now wouldn't you?"

"Yes'm."

"Sit there a while. Hold my hand."

"I will, mama. You rest now."

In late afternoon this second day she came to a creek and crossed it, carrying her shoes in one hand, her coat pulled up and bunched at the waist. Then she came back and again forded the stream, one of the suitcases riding at perilous balance on her head. The muddy bottom sucked at her feet. Green slime covered the rocks; she tried to avoid them. The water turned a thick brown where she walked. It trickled politely over the stones; up there a ways a skinny tree was down and twigs and leaves snagged on the skinny tree in the making of a forlorn dam. The stream swept at a good pace around it. There wouldn't be no beavers here. Beavers had better sense than to be in a place miserable as this. The woods here were thick and scraggly. Vines swept up over everything and hung still as ragged curtains from the trees. The earth was shaded, with pock holes scattered all over, each filled with an inch or two of water, and the creek was dark too, of an amber color. She got the second suitcase across, though she nearly lost it once when she slipped. Her grip gave way on the coat bunched at her waist and the coat got wet from the knees down; as she reached for it her sleeve unrolled and it too plopped into the water. At the bank she took off the coat and squeezed what she could from it. Then she put it on again. It was heavier now. The sleeve was cold and soggy against her wrist. She shivered, and stood a moment hugging herself.

Mud squished between her toes. She knelt at the water's edge and let the cool water flow over her feet. She put her hands under, marveling at how the slow current wanted to carry her hands along. Her stomach rumbled. She felt a wave of dizziness and knew she'd have to eat something soon. She should have spent some of her money for beans or a can of potted meat, but she hadn't been able to part with it. The prices alone was enough to make your gorge rise.

She thought of the cough drops in her pocket. Although here was food of a kind, she refrained from reaching for them. She'd never have put out good money for these cough drops herself. They'd been in her mama's shoulder purse, along with the hairpins and rumpled tissues, along with the comb and the teensy mirror in the fold-up case. The change purse had two dollars in it then, plus the change. It had her pills too, in a tiny brown bottle, only six left. Six gone to waste. She'd tried selling these back to the pharmacy man on the corner but he'd laughed at her. "How do I know you ain't spiked them pills?" he said. "How I know where in thunderation they been?" She'd insisted but he hadn't wilted an inch. The skinflint. Yes, you paid good money for a thing, it cost you an arm and a leg, but when you tried selling it back to these devils you found out how worthless it was. Those pills hadn't helped her mama. She'd said so herself a million times.

But you never knew. Those pills were now back in her mama's shiny black shoulder purse and the purse back in the suitcase. If ever she got to feeling run down the way her mama did then maybe she'd take them herself. Maybe they'd pep her up.

She examined her feet in the running water and wondered if she shouldn't wash her stockings now. They were bunched up wet around her ankles. She pulled them high again. They were streaked with mud, and stiff, nothing but pudding where her heels had bled. They had a zillion snags and runs. But there was no use now in opening up a suitcase and getting out another pair. In ten minutes they'd be as bad off as these. Best to wait until she got where she was going.

She cupped her hands into the water and drank. It dribbled between her fingers and down her chin. The water was cool, but tasted smoky somehow. It tasted burned. It didn't have the sparkle of city water. No telling what animals had dropped their leavings in it. Oh, but it was cool. She wiped wet hands over her face and neck and throat, for she was sweaty from all this carrying. Oh my, that felt good. Be nice to just dunk her head underwater. But the water stung her blisters; it pitched a fit at her sores. She winced, thinking maybe this was the worst pain. But it wasn't. The worse pain was all over now, including in her stomach where the water she'd drank weighed like an anvil.

She thought seriously about taking off her clothes and bathing herself all over; there might be some advantage in this. It didn't hurt you none, her mama said, to be clean. But the air had a nip in it. She didn't want to end up coughing and moaning the way her mama had. Her mama had smelled. She'd run the washcloth over her mama and pat on the pink powder but in a little while the smell came back again. A smell sort of like a hot ironing board. Her skin was dark too, like the cover you ironed on. Though her mama hadn't smelled it. She'd said, "No, no, don't open the window! Can't I at least rest in peace?"

Minnows swam at her feet. They'd shoot off a little way, then stop dead still, then dart off again. They hardly paid any attention now to her wriggling toes. She lifted her arms and sniffed under her armpits the way she'd at times seen her mama do. She couldn't smell anything. She didn't need no bath. To bathe here naked in the open would be next to foolishness. First thing you knew somebody'd be flying over in an airplane. Or some thief coming along. Anyway she'd never in her life bathed in full daylight. Bathing was for nighttime so you could go to sleep clean and dream nice pictures and wake up in the morning spick-and-span.

She looked hard at the suitcases. They'd got so heavy. My lifely goods, she thought. They weigh more than me. She wondered if maybe she couldn't lighten her load, maybe hide some of it away up here. Maybe take out the best things from the one case and stuff them in the other and go on along with that. She strode out of the creek, searching about for a good place. Maybe over there by that rotted stump. She'd never seen a place with so many stumps, or with so much rot. Some of it was black, too, like there had been a fire through here at some time. Long long ago, probably before she was born. Probably before her mama was born too. Before anybody was. Before there was this poor excuse for a lane or even spiders you could name it after. Probably a zillion years ago.

She saw no wheel tracks here and for an instant felt alarm. Had she somehow got off the main path? The tracks had come to be like company to her. But no, there they were, there they had been all the time. One set going one way, one going another. You could tell by how the horse hooves, if horse it was — mule maybe — left their prints in the ground. The one going was deeper; it had been carrying something. She wondered who had rode that wagon. Wondered if maybe it wasn't him. *Him*, yes, but she wouldn't say his name. It scared her even to think of him. What would he say when he saw her? Would he chase her off with a stick? *"Don't let him,"* her mama had said. *"You stand right up to him. Call him a jackal to his face, if that's what's come of him."*

She knelt over the bag before opening it; she listened, breath held, for any sound. Far off she saw a bird going. There was another one up in the big tree. Funny she hadn't seen it before. But she hadn't and maybe that meant there was a lot else she hadn't seen. Peeping Toms. Maybe this minute somebody was off in the bushes spying. Maybe him. Aw, heck no. That was foolishness. It looked more to her like no one was within a million miles. No one knew whether she was living or dead.

Everything was so still. Still and near to dead. She was going to have a hard time getting used to a quiet place like this. Even the creek bed seemed to feel it; its trickles were like little whispers over the stones.

"It's going to try me to my very eyeballs," she said aloud, just to give a voice to the place. "I don't know I can." Her voice shook. She laughed at herself.

She dragged both cases to the bushes at the side of the lane. She worked carefully and quickly, sorting out the goods, exchanging articles contained in one for articles in the other. Her mama's high-heeled pumps delayed her a bit. She placed the soft leather up to her cheek, her eyes closed. Closed and wet. Her mama had loved these pumps. She'd hardly worn them at all, loving them that much. She had a dozen clear memories of her mama in these pumps. Her mama had such beautiful legs. Ankles thin as her wrists and her hips lovely as a moving picture lady. Your heart went up to your throat when you thought of mama in these pumps. You'd think heads would snap off the way men turned theirs when mama went by. "Oh, mama, damn you," she said. "Oh, damn you." She wiped the coat sleeve against her eyes and took bitter sight on these high heels. Her mama had bought these for dancing first: *"I needed new pumps to go with my dress. Do you like them? You don't mind my leaving you alone? You go to sleep early and I promise I'll tell you everything went on when I come in."* Her mama danced in these shoes, but only that once. They were hardly worn; not a scuff any place. She saw her mama at the long mirror, turning, looking down at one lifted leg. Then turning and lifting the other. *"Are they straight, honey? My seams? Aren't they pretty with these new pumps? Am I pretty enough, do you think, to be seen in this world? You can come with us if you want to. Monty won't mind."*

She bit her lips, told herself to stop this. "Stop it," she said. "Stop this sniveling like a backward child. You quit it right now."

She'd take these pumps with her. Best be on the safe side. She'd take this silver mirror too, and the jewel box. She'd take these framed pictures of herself and her mama. Take these fancy scarves. These white gloves that went all the way up to her elbow. In these gloves wasn't mama grand!

She crushed down the lid and after an effort got it snapped. Both sides were stuffed out fat. She couldn't lift the bag. Oh heavy, too heavy. She stood up straight, screeching silently at the weight. She kicked the ground in fury and tried again. She strained, applying both hands, tongue between her teeth, crossing her eyes, and got it an inch or two off the ground. Hopeless. How could a few doodads weigh so much? It beat her. "It beats me," she said. "I'm stumped." The attempt made her giddy. It made her pulse race. She felt a flush of scarlet on her face and half sat, half tumbled down. Her knees shook. She let her head fall between her legs; she watched the ground undulate. The taste of bile charged up her throat. She couldn't stop the quivering in her legs. Her eyes refused to focus. Her face was hot and she slapped a hand up over her eyes, thinking: I've got what mama had. I've got a fever to beat the band. Her head swam. Was this how mama had felt? Her heartbeat was racing, she could hear it going clippity clop. Yesterday? Was it yesterday morning she'd eaten the last dregs of what was in the icebox and poured out a bottle of milk that had turned? Gurgle-gurgle. She'd had saltine crackers and a smear of peanut butter left in the jar. She could see that clearly, the empty jar, but not where that was. She could see the man with the cigarette dangling and the four bus lights blinking against the dark. She could see the white apple the man across from her had and in her hunger she almost reached for it. *Did* reach for it, or for something, because a second later the apple spun away and bus too and in its place, head lowered between her legs, there was just her own hand wildly scratching in the dirt. I've slipped off the deep end, she thought, like that sister my daddy had. My yo-yo's come loose. Was she so hungry she'd now eat dirt? She half remembered a time when she had. As a baby she had. So her mama said. "You and dirt! You'd have stuffed wiggling beetles in your jaws if I hadn't kept you from it!" "Where was *he*, then?" "Him? Your papa? He was long gone. Or I was. You'd have had to chain me up like a dog to keep me out there." "What's he like? Did you ever see him again?" "Oh, once or twice. He come around. But our feelings for each other were all dead and buried by that time. I didn't know him from Adam, and wanted him less." "Would he know me now?" "Know you? Well, maybe he would. When you cry, when you want something bad and can't have it, you both have that hungdog miserable look. I reckon he might recognize that."

She got the bags sorted to her satisfaction. That one she was leaving behind she carried up through the woods, over a marsh that slurped at her heels; she hid the case away behind bramble bushes at the edge of a wide, untended, gullied field. She threw dead brush up over the hiding place. The bag looked safe enough there. She circled the spot, eyeing it from every angle, and pronounced herself satisfied. "Take a hawk's eye to find it," she said. "Anyway, I don't mean it to stay for long."

Something pricked at her ankle. She looked down with a screech. A black tick had its nose buried in her flesh. She picked it off, then saw another between her toes and rubbed her toes over the earth to erase the itch. She felt something crawling lightly, ticklishly, over her neck and she whirled in a fury, clawing with her fingers there. In a moment she was scratching herself all over, scrambling back through the marsh, feeling ticks all over. They were black ugly things and came loose with little tufts of white skin clinging to them. A pair of startled quail shot up in a sudden flurry of wings, startling her. In an instant other groups burst out of nearby bush and weed and cut in a swift, curving line through the sky. They circled high and disappeared. A crow cawed somewhere. She heard the rattle of something else too, uneven and distant, an echo perhaps, and stood stock-still, cupping hands to one ear. It came again, a rumble this time. She darted free of the marsh, zigzagging out, the long coat yanked up to her waist and flapping. She dropped quickly down into a spread of weeds. It sounded like a wagon. It sounded like someone coming, to her. "Goddamnit," she whimpered, "I ain't ready yet."

For a long time, flat in the weeds, her head raised, she didn't move but stayed alert to all sounds, her muscles taut, her breath shallow and quick. What if it's him? she thought. What if he sees my suitcase on that road? What if it's stole, or he's got a gun and shoots me dead? She considered leaping up, racing back to the lane, yanking her suitcase off into the bush. But she couldn't take the chance. She didn't want to meet him like this, not in no woods and looking like a rat. She would meet him, had to, but not like this, like some brainless waif hiding in the woods, not knowing doodly-squat.

No further sound came. There was only stillness over the place. "There ain't nothing," she whispered at last. "I imagined that noise." Finally she got up, dusted off her clothes, searched her legs and arms for ticks, and returned in a run to the lane.

Nothing had changed. There her suitcase was and the babbling creek, nothing coming either up or down the lane. I dreamt up that wagon, she thought. I surely did. To calm herself she stepped her bare feet into the creek's cold water. Her mama had told her how to go about it: "You walk right up to his door," she said. "You hold your head high, too; I don't want him thinking I didn't know how to raise you. You watch out for dogs; he'll have those. You knock and when he comes you tell him who you are. You tell him what's gone on here. What's come of me. You tell him it's his turn now." She'd made it sound so easy, her mama had. But she hadn't told her it would take days and days and a million miles to get her there. She hadn't said nothing about how soon a full belly could start rubbing backbone. She'd have to eat something soon; she couldn't go on like this.

She stared down at the tranquil water at her feet. There was white sand washed up in this spot. The water was clear, numbing to her legs. Her legs looked split, like she'd stepped out of her bones. She flexed her toes, grimacing at the icy waves. "What if he don't want me?" she said. "What if he says I can go rot in hell?" Her mama hadn't answered that. Her mama, poor thing, had moaned and coughed and slept.

Minnows swam lazily at her feet, looking silvery in the light. Her body threw a zigzag shadow as she bent her face to the surface. A minnow was a fish. A person could eat fish. The minnows veered away as she lowered her hands into the water. Then they reassembled to drift somnolently between her fingers and legs. Her stomach growled; her mouth moistened. She reckoned people had eaten worse. Babies gnawed at crib paint and didn't always die from it. In the picture show, seated beside her mama, she'd seen ritzy people eating frog legs. That would be a whole lot worse. Once her own mama had cooked what she called brains, and made her taste it. She didn't reckon minnows could kill her.

She cupped her hands together and brought them up ever so slowly. Mostly they drifted free. Those few trapped in her hands shook their tails as the water dribbled away; then they stretched flat and still against her skin, looking so much smaller than they had in the water.

Eyes closed, making a face, she licked her palms clean. She

swallowed without chewing and imagined she felt them flopping about inside her empty stomach.

She was stooping to gather up more when she heard the sudden clop of hooves, the creak of wagon wheels. She caught her breath and with a low cry dashed out of the water. She swept up her suitcase, swung it, and went tumbling behind it into the dense thicket at the side of the road. She burrowed herself down.

A wagon came into sight, empty and rattling, pulled by a mule, which walked with its head low and bobbing, bobbing and swaying. The mule was old and tired, dust-colored, its knees bald; yellow pus dripped from its eyes; as it neared she could see flies crawling over the pus. It was chewing at the bit in its mouth and swishing its tail.

At the stream the mule stopped and drank. It made big slurping noises and once or twice flung its head around. One of its ears didn't stand up.

When it was done drinking it clumped in its traces, edging off twisty from the wagon to munch on tall weeds.

"Well, Buddyroll?" the man said.

He had a whispery, gentle voice.

The man in the wagon was standing, the reins secured by a hand tucked by thumb into his waist. He was idly surveying the stream, content apparently to let the animal loiter and graze. Was this him? She did not think it could be. Her mama had said he'd be a good height and thin and pretty nice-looking. He'd have a certain glint in his eyes that would make a woman go goose bumpy. He'd have a way about him that let you know he meant to get what he wanted and that you wouldn't mind it. *"That man whispered things in my ear I'll carry to my grave,"* her mama had said. *"I think sometimes of what he said to me and my hair still stands up. He could make a mummy's eyes pop out."* Mama must of been joshing, for this one was nothing. He was red-dirt nothing. He had a big fat gut and muscley arms all stubby. He wore a rumpled greasy felt hat

pushed back on his head. You could see where the brim had
shaded his face so the sun burned his nose and left red swatches
all across his face. It was an ugly face. He had a stick in his
mouth, moving it from side to side. He had bulgy jaws and
meaty ears and a thick, streaked neck. His little pig eyes
gleamed. No, this wasn't him. It couldn't be. Mama didn't have
memory to beat a bat.

She saw him unbutton his pants and lift out his thing. He
peed in a long wide arch into the stream. He had big calloused
sunburned hands and sunburned arms and a red nose, but his
weasel was puny and white. It looked like hardly nothing a
human would want. He'd be better off not peeing at all than
showing that thing. He shook it, bent his knees, and loaded it
back inside. Him? The idea was so funny she almost laughed
out loud. He wouldn't have sense to beat a cockroach. Him?
The likelihood was plain disgusting. Her mama would never
have let herself curl up to nothing looking like that.

He said something in a low voice to the mule, which turned
and looked at him coldly. He hopped down and removed the bit
from the animal's mouth. The mule rippled its haunches and
went back to its feeding. It ripped up a tall growth of grass by
the roots and ate it down to the dirt. It scraped the dirt off
against a bald knee, then ate the roots. The man knelt by the
stream, lacing a hand through the water. He pulled a rag from
his pocket and wet it. He wiped the rag behind and around his
neck. He dipped the rag again into the water and crossed over to
the mule. The mule had an open puckered sore high on a hind
leg. The man cleansed it. The mule swished him in the face a
time or two, and rippled his skin again, and again the man said
something to him.

Buddyroll quit, it sounded like.

He put the bit back into the animal's mouth and hopped up
into the wagon. He gave a small shake to the reins and
sluggishly the mule responded. The wagon rattling started
again. The man took off his hat as they crossed the stream, and

swatted it against his leg. Dust flew up. The hatband had cut a line in his forehead, leaving a strip of white skin there. White and freckly. He didn't have much hair. What there was was reddish. She felt her face heat up, noticing this. His red hair, if you could believe mama, was where she'd got hers. He was how come she'd got her freckles, too.

He seemed to be smiling at something as the wagon creaked by, the smile slack on his face, as if he didn't know it to be there.

Her stomach rumbled. She shifted in her hiding spot, ramming a fist up against her stomach to quieten the emptiness.

"Damn son of a bitch," she said. "If he's mine I don't claim him."

Ahead, the road dipped and curved; it rose on to higher ground. A bit yonder from that point, trailing at a distance, she saw the wagon turn into a rutted yard.

He went on down the path, through an open fence gate at the rear of the house, to a weathered, leaning barn.

The house was as her mama said it would be.

A wide porch extended over the full length of the two front rooms, with two worn cane-bottom chairs tilted to the wall, and a wooden swing on chains that, except in summer, lifted the swing up to the ceiling. Two windows faced the lane, divided in the middle by a sagging pinewood door, the screen part open. Behind the front rooms, he'd added a hallway and two other rooms. He'd lived here, so her mama said, with a sick sister who hadn't taken lightly another woman's presence on the place. But the sister had passed on, her mama said. She'd died of craziness, if not boredom. An old sycamore, with a maze of thick graceful limbs, shaded one half of the yard. A stump across from it showed where another had been. A stone chimney went up at the side, and a bent weather vane with a rooster at the top guarded the roof of the house. She saw how he'd patched the tin roof with flattened-out cans. He'd put in a new windowpane not long before.

The place had lights now; it hadn't had electricity in her mama's time.

She was about to step up on the porch and peek through the windows when she heard him coming. He was whistling. She ducked low over the grass, hit the lane, and took off running. For the balance of the day she searched out the place, avoiding open fields, steering wide of his house. In the afternoon she crawled up in a tangle of vines and slept, pulling the black coat up over her head. It seemed to her she slept a long time but when she rubbed her eyes awake the same bird was alight, alight but silent, preening its feathers, on the same high limb. It was so blessed still out here even the birds had caught it. You couldn't hardly breathe because the earth seemed to want to sop it up like gravy on a plate. Her body itched all over. Her flesh was covered with bites, with scratches and welts. Bruises, head to toe. She took off her shoes and picked briars off the bottoms of her feet. They were black and swollen up some. You couldn't even see any more where the blisters had been; it was all raw now. She rolled the stockings down, gritting her teeth, wincing, as she peeled them away from the dried blood on her heels. That was the worst pain, these heels. These feet. These scratches and cuts and being stuck out here. Standing, she felt dizzy, and had to sit down again. Her head swirled. I've got what mama had, she thought. I'm going to waste away in these ungodly woods and go to my grave out here. She picked a black tick out of her scalp and flattened it between her two thumb-nails. When mama went down she'd wanted to go down with her. She'd wanted to be shut up with her and have the lid closed on them. They'd said no, no you can't, but it seemed to her this had happened anyway. It was happening now. The lid was closing, but mama wasn't raising her arms to welcome her. Mama was stretched out flat, not saying anything. Come along, child. Come along, child. Mama's back was turned or she wasn't there at all: black space, cold black air, that's all mama was. She hadn't cried then, with mama being lowered down. She could have and wanted to but she hadn't because mama made her so mad. She hadn't wanted to be mad, not at mama, but she was so she just bit her lip and hung on, and if anybody spoke to her or touched her she moved away from them. She hated how they whispered, as if her mama could hear. She kept moving away and they kept coming with her until more of them were huddled with her up by the tree than were down there by the tent where her mama was. She didn't know why they'd come in the first place. Nobody had asked them to. They had no right to be there. She shook when they touched her. She threw off their hands and had to edge away. She had to go on up as far as the tree, but still they kept coming with her. Sniveling, fluttering up little hankies to the nose. What she wanted was for her and her mama to be alone. Not being alone with mama, that last time, that was the worst pain. It was worse than bloody heels and that man on the bus with a cigarette dangling between his lips. It was worse than spending good money to come out here to this dismal daddy in this dismal place. In the end it was her mama alone. You couldn't blame mama for turning her back on her, for changing into black space, into cold black air that never answered a word you said. She felt dizzy now, and hot, and knew this was her mama's sweat on her brow. "I won't talk to you, child, but you can have that. I give my fever to you, along with everything else." Hunger wasn't doing this to her. Hunger wasn't worth talking about, because she had money in her pocket and could buy food, lots of it, any time she wanted to. She could eat weeds, like that mule. She could eat these cough drops in her coat pocket, but she wouldn't. Her mama had said, "Go to the store and buy me these cough drops to ease my throat, and get some little treat for yourself," and she'd done so, but her mama hadn't touched them. Her mama's eyes had rolled in her head. You could take her hand in your own hand and squeeze but her mama couldn't squeeze your own hand back. She'd sleep and you'd sit by the bed thinking how beautiful she was. You'd hold her hand and your own hand would burn. You'd watch her eyes move under the lids sunken and dark. You'd watch the tremor in her lips and dab a wet cloth over them for they were always dry. Sweat broke out on her brow and you could fold a cold wet cloth over her but the cloth got hot as fire in a minute and in the meantime the fever just went on elsewhere. She'd wake and cough and say, "I didn't doze off did I?" "Can you eat, mama?" you'd say. "Can I bring you anything? Are you feeling better?" She'd pat your hand and try to smile. It broke your heart how she tried to smile and that was the worst pain. It was worse than blisters or having your belly gnaw or coming this far for nothing. Worse was what was back there, though it wasn't back there but with you every minute, which was what made it worse. Worse was mama not squeezing your hand after you'd squeezed hers first and then that hand not being there to squeeze although you could still feel her hand in yours. Worse was waiting for the squeeze to come and knowing now it wouldn't. "Mama, can I fetch you something? Can I rub your back or freshen them sheets?"

"Not now, child."

"All right, mama."

"Don't you be weary on my account, baby."

"All right, mama."

You could put your hand behind mama's head and lift her up; you could put a spoon between her lips and feed her like a baby. I loved bathing mama's feet. You could run a damp, cool cloth between her toes and sometimes that would make her smile. "You can turn the light off now," she'd say, and you'd go over and pretend to do it, not letting her know it was plain daylight and no lamp burning. She'd lean on you those days when she could cross the room, and she'd lean on you, coming back. "My right arm," she'd say, "is a pretty little girl. She's my left arm, too." Her lips would tremble when the real pains came and she'd turn her face against the pillow so you couldn't see it. You couldn't get a doctor to come. You'd call up on the store phone and they'd say do this, do that, and you tore home and did it but it didn't help none. You fed her pills by the pail but that didn't help none. "Does it help, mama? Does it relax you? Can you sleep now?"

"Oh, child. Oh Oh Oh. Oh, I feel like I've gone in the oven headfirst. Pull me out now. Grab my legs and pull. Putting a body headfirst into the fiery furnace is the one sure way they've found of making sure no ghosts lag behind. I feel my ghost has burned and the rest has yet to follow. You take my coat. You take my purse and my nice scarves and my new shoes. You take all the fine stockings the navy sees fit to give me."

The navy. You had to smile, thinking about that. You had to laugh out loud. Even her mama in her worse sickness could. One of her mama's old boyfriends, Monty his name was, sent these stockings to her. He got them from Ship's Store or foreign ports or off the black market and in they came, regular as rainwater. "I'm being swept off my feet by nylons," her mama would say. "It beats me what men will do. Why I only went out with that sailorman once! I let him hold me tight on the dance floor, but dancing was all. I liked his arms around me. I let him kiss and hold me when his leave was up and I dashed down to see him when he left on the train. I pulled him back against the red-brick wall and I was the one held him that time. That time I was the one raining the kisses down. 'You come back,' I said. He said he'd write, but what I said was, 'Well you know how sailors are.' I should have given myself to him. God knows, it's little enough. If his ship goes down and he doesn't return I'll cry and wish a thousand times I had. I think of that each time his nylons come. I think of it each time I pull one on."

Men loved her mama. Two had fought over her once, but she'd never spoken to either again.

"I won't be treated like I'm a lump of clay that they can mold and take and have. I didn't care a snake for either of them and they'd of saved themselves a heap of bruised knuckles had they asked me first.

"Your father wasn't that way," she said. "He never fought

for me or raised a word to stop me when I said I was leaving that place. It wasn't him I was leaving, as I saw it. Only that place. He never so much as said 'Please' or 'Don't do it.' I know he was unhappy and cried, because his sister, crazy as she was, came one day and told me. She said 'Come back and this time I'll try to be good.' But your father didn't try to sway me. You can't lock up wind, he said. He said he wouldn't try to tame it either.''

Several times in her wanderings the girl caught sight of her father as he moved from barn to shed or shed to house. Once, she spotted him on the rear doorstep, calmly surveying the horizon. In late afternoon he came out and scattered feed from a bucket to a half-dozen chickens that flew down from trees. He appeared later with a pail and followed a footpath down to where two sows wallowed in muddy puddles inside a pen. Afterward, she saw him carrying in wood. Another time he was out by the fence gate, whittling on something.

She didn't see any dogs. She saw something streak across his yard once, but couldn't tell what it was.

For long intervals, when he disappeared inside the house, she lay flat in this or that field watching his back door.

Down beyond the fenced-off area was an orchard; she trampled about there, but what little fruit remained on the ground was wormy and rotten. A space of ground nearer the house had served as his garden in seasons past. She pulled a young carrot out of the soil and ate it quickly; she searched a long time for others but found nothing.

On toward nightfall, troubled by the rising cold, she followed what seemed to be an ancient path, trampled down in parts, in parts wild again, and eventually found herself regarding an abandoned, burned-out site inside a ring of scorched trees. Someone had lived here. Wrinkled sheets of tin roofing, blackened boards and black jacknife timbers covered the area. Bushes sprouted midst the rubble. In one corner, climbing up over a wall that remained partially intact, honeysuckle was taking over. She eyed that wall. She eyed the tin. She could fashion a roof of some kind where that wall was, and spend the night here.

She set to work clearing out that space. She worked on into dark, scarcely noticing she had.

The little room she erected was well-hidden; you'd have to stand right up on it to know it was there. She had room for her suitcases and room to stretch out, though not stand up. She put in an opening at the front big enough so that she might crawl through.

She could hide here, she thought, for a million years.

Afterward, she lugged her suitcases up from the woods. She rested then in the cramped shelter, peering up at the streaks and pinpoints of night sky. For a few minutes she slept, although she did not intend to.

Later in the night she worked her way down to the creek and there, trembling with cold, washed herself. Like ice, the water was. It made her teeth chatter and her bones crunch up tight. But it felt good to be clean. It was like heaven, getting the soot and filth off her. She slipped naked into her coat, rolling up the dirty clothes under her arm. She hastened back to her shelter among the ruins and for long minutes sat shivering, waiting for warmth to return. She didn't think about hunger now. Being cold is the worse ache, she told herself. I've never known nothing worse than cold. Being alone in the world was a glory ride compared to being cold. If I stop shivering it will just go away. But she couldn't stop shivering. Her skin was so white and shaky she could see it even in this black hole. Her scalp itched; her hair was grimy, too; tomorrow in fresh daylight she'd go and wash that.

She felt about inside the suitcase for a pair of stockings — a new pair — and pulled them on. "Bless the navy," she said, for this was what her mama liked to say. "Him with his nylons, going to sweep me off my feet." She drew the hose up over her hips and tucked the extra length inside her panties. Her mama had kept hers up with garter belts or she'd rolled and twisted them somehow and they'd stayed up. Beautiful legs, old mama had. She felt about for a sweater and skirt and slipped these on. She got out a comb and raked that through her tangly hair, making low cries as the comb pulled. She wondered where her bow had got to. She rubbed a finger over her teeth and moistened that finger and set a shape to her eyebrows. She painted her lips with the tube her mama had said she could have. She rouged her cheeks the way her mama had showed her how.

She took out her money and hid it away inside a suitcase.

She hooked the purse over her arm and crawled out of her hole.

In the beginning the house was but a faint speck of yellow light low on the horizon, obscured now and then by the land's undulations. She crossed the fields with short bursts of speed, swinging her shoes in her hands, using his lighted window as her guide. Soon the house was outlined in full, with the sagging roof and the bent weather vane and the big sycamore at the front.

She crouched down where his last field stopped, from there inching her way forward. Smoke wafted up from the chimney; the light was flickering. He passed by the window once and she ducked down, holding her breath. She could hear faint sounds from inside and wondered whether he had visitors, maybe a woman. She wondered what her mama would say about that. Or maybe her mama was wrong about the sister being dead the way she was about him having dogs. But it sounded to her like music; it sounded like a radio.

She raised her eyes above the sill. He was seated on a log stool before the fire, whittling on a piece of wood, a carving of some kind. He was seated on a log although the room held plenty of nice easy chairs and an old settee that looked comfortable. It surprised her how clean and orderly everything was. The floor was of polished wood, a nice deep color, with numerous old clocks on the wall and nice pictures, and lacy antimacassars on the arms of the settee and chairs. It was a whole lot better-looking place than she would have thought, and lots better and more roomy than the place she and her mama had. Her mama hadn't been one for keeping things straight, and she hadn't either.

She didn't see no sister. She didn't see no tramp layabout girl friend either.

His shirt was unbuttoned. He had a curly ring of hair on his chest and clean hands and what looked to her like greenish eyes.

He had a drink in a glass down on the floor beside him and now he drank from that. He took three or four deep swallows.

An alcoholic, she thought. If he ain't alcoholic then my name is Clementine.

He was patting his foot to music. The music didn't come from a radio, but from an old Victrola over in the corner. The lid was up and she could see a fat silvery arm spinning over the phonograph record. She'd seen Victrolas like that in town with a big white spotted dog beside them.

She knew that song. It was an old one. Her mama had hummed it sometimes.

"You're his only daughter," her mama had said. "You go to him. I mean it, now."

She moved around the house and clumped noisily up onto the porch. She stretched up her stockings and brushed at her coat. She took a deep breath and knocked on his door.

"I'll try it," she said. "I'll give him twenty-four hours to prove himself."

Why the Heathens Are No More

MY FOLKS TOLD ME that if I left my room things would begin to happen to me. I'd get some life in me. "It's no fun sitting around the house all day," they said. "What do you think about in there? You haven't even bothered to get your radio repaired. What you ought to do is put on one of those pretty dresses, fix your face, and go out and meet someone. Someone nice. Honey, we hate to see you like this. Or you could work on your education, go back to school. We're not saying you have to push to be a doctor or a teacher, nothing hard. We just think you should get out of the house. Show a little spirit. We don't know what's the matter with you. You're driving us nuts."

They said this to me a thousand times a day. Finally I went out. But nothing happened.

"Suzy!" my mother said. "You were only gone half an hour!"

It seemed to me more like three. What I did was walk the blocks down to where the park is, then crossed the park, eyeing a few children at the swings, and I went on from there to where my old boyfriend used to live. The place looks all shut up now, but it used to be Richard's house. Richard was my boyfriend back three or four years ago when I was twelve. We went to the movies a few times. We never even held hands. It didn't occur to us.

"Where did you go?" my mother asked. "What happened?

How did you get that blotch on your dress? You should be more careful.''

"I went by Richard's house," I said.

"Richard? Who's Richard?"

That night I heard the two of them talking. My dad said, "It's a start, I guess. It's something."

Mom said it wasn't normal. I needed a doctor.

"Now don't start up about doctors. With what's been spent on doctors in this house people could start up railroads. They could span the continent."

The rest I missed because they started whispering. I guess they were worried I was listening.

I didn't leave the house again for some time. I hardly ever left my room. I didn't have the energy. There didn't seem to be much point in it. Where could I go? It was nicer sitting in my room.

Several times I heard my mother on the phone. She shouts, thinking people can't hear her. Maybe they can't. I haven't had much experience with telephones. People have called me maybe ten times in my life. Most of those times I haven't said much. Frankly, I'd as soon we didn't have one.

"What do you mean what brought this on?" my mother said. "Nothing brought this on. She was always the silent type. But she was like any other normal girl. Nothing brought it on. She's being difficult, that's all. She's doing it to hurt us."

I had to smile at that. Hurt them why? It wouldn't have occurred to me. They were nice loving parents, about all you could ask for. They were all I'd ever known. I wouldn't want anyone better. All I wished was that they'd both get on with their lives, stop worrying about me. What was wrong with me shutting myself up in my room? I bet a lot of people did it. If you took a poll, I bet such people would number in the thousands. What harm were we doing? Why was it so upsetting? It was upsetting to me, too, how they complained, but I didn't let on. When they spoke to me I gave a sad little smile and shrugged, maybe to show them I didn't know why. That it wasn't any big deal.

Mostly I slept. I slept about eighteen hours a day, no set times, whenever I felt like it. Sometimes nice deep sleeps and other times little easy nice ones. I hardly ever dreamed. Once in a while I'd have a real harsh time of it, thinking I saw someone with an ax about to chop off my tongue, and once in a while there was something like a Roto Rooter going at my plumbing, but it, they, didn't mean anything. It was only a dream. My interest in dreams was practically nil. Sometimes I wished I had my radio fixed, and different curtains, but that was all. The stations didn't come in very well anyway. Who needed all that noise? Richard, before he went away, said he liked those on the edge best. Those that came in for a moment, then got pushed out. There was one spot on the dial, he said, where you got about six stations at once. They'd crackle and spit at each other; for long minutes you wouldn't hear any at all. He'd sit me down on his bed, he'd say, "You wait. Pretty soon they are going to go at it again. You're going to think it's a full-scale war. They think it is all so important, you see. They think they've got something to tell us that we must know. Hear that one? That music? That's the little brother of the six. It's about two thousand watts and has got its transformer up on a hill. They thought it would solve their problems, but I guess it's too windy up there. That's in the day. In the night it's totally different at this spot on the dial. Some lady from Sioux City comes on. She talks and she talks. She talks about 'Our Lord.' 'Hello, heathens!' she says. 'Oh you, heathens! Are you ready, heathens? Are you ready for Our Lord? Get down on your knees, heathens! Repeat after me, heathens!' She's pretty wonderful. For a quarter and a self-addressed stamped envelope she'll send you every word she says. 'Ask for Booklet Two Thousand. Send it to HEATHENS, Sioux City, 51104.'" Richard was always sending his quarters all over the place. He kept what came locked up behind a Yale lock in this wooden chest.

For a quarter he'd pull one out. But he'd not often let you touch these documents with your hands. "No way," he'd say. "I'm collecting irreplaceable goods. These items are going to be my future."

My mother went on and on about doctors. One morning she said, "Today's the day. Put on your shoes. Wash your face. Let's go.

"Don't worry," she said. "It's only for a checkup. People have them all the time. It won't kill you."

A checkup for staying in your room? I told her the doctor would die laughing.

"Hush," she said. "Get out of the car. I wish you hadn't worn those clothes. I feel ashamed, being with you."

The doctor said I was fine. She said I was in excellent health. A little run-down, she said. "All this girl needs is a lot of rest."

After that speech my mother disappeared into her office for a long time. They both came out sour-faced. I thought I was in for it, but as it happened neither spoke to me. My mother didn't look my way till she had driven us practically home.

"That takes the cake," she then said. "I don't know what games you're playing. That high-and-mighty bitch wouldn't tell me what you two said in there. All I can say is I better not ever learn you've been blaming me. You better shape up. You're not too old to get my hand in your face."

Neither she nor my father spoke to me for three days. They gave me cold looks. I had no idea what they thought I'd been doing. I kept my curtains pulled. After they'd gone to bed I'd come out and get an apple or two. I stacked the cores up in a saucer, building a little house. Before long, the ants were all over them. They came up in a line on the wall, one after the other. They left by the floor, hauling along chunks of dried apple.

And they wondered what I found to do in there.

One night my father came in and sat on my bed.

"How's it going, honey?" he said.

I told him I was writing in my diary, I was writing to Richard.

"Who's Richard?"

"Richard's my boyfriend."

He laughed.

"I was talking to John Yanks today," he said. "You remember John?"

I had never heard this name before in my life.

"Sure, you remember John Yanks. He used to be around here all the time."

"I must have been over at Richard's," I said.

He looked at me strangely for a long time. Then he laughed again, but it was a put-on laugh. "Anyway," he said, "John and me put our heads together. He's got a scheme. He needs your help."

"I'm sleepy," I said. "I want to go to bed now." If John Yanks or anybody else needed my help, they were in a very bad way. They were far worse off than me.

"He's got a job for you," he said. "Decent pay. Minimum wage, but you don't have the experience. You'll enjoy it. Are you listening?"

I stopped looking at my hands and looked at him. He looked old. It seemed he'd aged ten years since I'd last had a long close look at him.

"Good," he said. He patted my hands. "That's my girl. You're going to pull out of this. You've got a lot of good people on your side. We're counting on you."

I could hardly keep my eyelids up. I tried closing my hands, but couldn't.

Then he turned the light off and left. I heard the two of them in their bedroom whispering together. "That'll be the day," I heard my mother say.

I put my flashlight beam on the ants. There were fewer of

them now. I moved an apple core over by the wall, nearer their exit, but they didn't show much interest. They went on by it, to the saucer.

Kind of stupid, I thought.

The backside of my radio had a label on it saying "No User-Serviceable Parts. For servicing refer to qualified personnel." I poked around inside with a nail file, but it was nothing doing. The radio hadn't worked since a few days after Richard gave it to me. This was one evening when he'd been trying to get the heathen lady to come in. He'd thumped it a few times with the heel of his hand. He was quite upset. "She must have been taken off the air," he said. "The heathens got to her. I've been expecting it." He sat moping, toying with a set of keys he carried in his pocket. He was very sad and wouldn't go to the movies with me. "You know," he said, "one day the heathens are going to take over unless somebody does something about it."

"What can be done?" I said. "Isn't it hopeless?"

He looked alarmed. He looked mad. "Are you crazy?" he said. "You sound like everyone else! You sound like a heathen yourself!"

I felt he was picking on me. I told him to stop it.

"*She* was doing something about it," he said. "That lady in Sioux City. Maybe you think she was just out to convert the rednecks. Maybe you think it was only religion she was going on about. If that's so, you've got it wrong. She crossed all tracks. She didn't care beans about getting idiots into heaven."

I didn't say anything. Richard was excitable and sometimes he got so hepped up he looked dangerous.

"Here, you take it," he said, meaning the radio. "I don't even want it any more. Radio isn't going to get the job done anyway."

"What job?" I said.

We put on our coats and he walked me partway home. He

stopped at the corner, not wanting to go any farther. It was where he always stopped. "I don't get it," he said.

"Get what, Richard?"

"Why she's off the air. She was really good. I've been corresponding with her."

"You have?" I felt a little jealous. Richard had a lot of correspondence with people I'd never so much as heard of.

"Well," he said. "I'll look into it. One thing I know is that she hasn't given up. I told her about my vision, you see. She was very impressed. She said it could move mountains."

I asked what vision, but he was deep in thought and didn't reply. He went on home without giving any more notice to me.

My mother was in a vile mood after the doctor's chat. She harped at me and my father said, "Let her alone, darling. It only makes matter worse."

"You could at least help us with dinner," she said. "Get in here. Peel the potatoes....Oh not like that. Oh forget it, you're useless. Go back to your room."

John Yanks showed up. They sat in the living room with drinks that might have been made out of peanut butter. "I could use her," John Yanks said. "Only I'm not claiming she would like it."

John Yanks smiled a lot. He smiled all the time.

"It's insane," mother said. "She falters, just crossing the room."

"Hard on the legs," John Yanks said. "If you're not used to it. She'll get aching feet."

"Just what she needs," said my father. "Force her out in the world, make her meet people. She's got to snap out of it. Who's going to look after her after we're dead?"

"Thanks," mother said.

"So long as we understand each other," John Yanks told them. "So long as you think she can do it."

"Nothing to it," father said. "She's clever. She can handle it."

"She's in a fog," mother said. "You're both crazy."

"Nope, not much glamor in this job," John Yanks said.

"Be good for her," father said.

"What's her trouble exactly?" asked John Yanks. "Maybe you'd be better off taking her to a doctor."

"Doctors!" said mother.

"Shhhh," father said. "I heard a board creak. I think she's listening."

The boards had creaked all right. They creaked because I had got sleepy. I was going back to my room.

"Suzy!" they called. "Come and meet Mr. Yanks!"

I didn't answer. I crawled into bed. There is something so nice about sleeping. I loved it.

I tried remembering some of the pictures Richard and I had seen, but none were memorable. Richard had always made me pay his way. "I'll go if you want to," he'd say, "but don't think I'm wasting my money on junky movies. Six months from now you won't remember a single one of them."

I doted on movies; I could lose myself in movies.

There came a time when he wouldn't go with me at all. "I guess you'd rather stay in your room and think your thoughts," I told him. "I guess you think your precious heathens are more fun than being with me."

"Grow up, Suzy," he said. "Use your mind, why don't you?"

He pulled out this big box from under his bed. He got out his keys. The box was filled with old newspapers and tattered magazines; it was stuffed with charts and graphs he'd worked on over the years. "Look at these," he said. "Try to get a grip on what's been happening in this world."

I flipped through some of them. There were a lot of horrible pictures of people lying dead on streets and byways and in open fields. There were children with ugly black rifles in their hands. There were mass graves and corpses with no flesh left on them. There were three boys dead in a gravel pit. There were mushroom clouds and a lot of black type making you think of the end of the world. Much of it was in foreign languages: tract upon tract of dense text that looked dreary and boring.

"That's heathen work," he said. "Government policy, in many instances. Your 'Special of the Month.' What's coming at you today. Take some. Take it home, brush up on the facts. I'm done with that part. It's yours now, a gift. Wait here, I'll get you a bag."

"But these are in French, Richard. Here are some in German. I can't read these languages, Richard."

"So study," he said. "Lay off your stupid movies. Get your nose down into the heathens' file. The thing about heathens is that they are never who you think they are."

"Who are they?" I said.

"Look!" he said. He was really getting mad. His face was red and he was pacing the room, hopping about. Each time I tried getting up he zapped forward and shoved me back down. "Don't ask me that," he said. "How do I know? You don't know either. Nobody knows until they are practically dead. Then it's too late. You can look back at the people in your life and say so-and-so was, and so-and-so, and about a million others. But then it's too late to go out and crack heads. Or you may find on your deathbed that you led a pretty heathenish life yourself. That's why that Sioux City woman chose the blanket approach. It's why she went at everyone. 'Oh you heathens!' she said. 'If you're not a heathen, then declare yourself. Let's see some proof. Don't give me any of that holier-than-thou shit or quote me your biblical jive. We got a million little popes spewing out their mumbo this, their jumbo that. Heathendom! Heathendom!' Well, you heard her. You know how she worked."

"Richard," I said. "Oh, Richard."

I told him I didn't understand. I told him he was sounding crazy to me. This wounded him. His eyes got wet. His lips trembled and his knees shook. He couldn't keep his hands still. I tried standing up and he rabbit punched me. "Sit down," he said. "Maybe I am. It's the risk we take, no question of that. I don't mind admitting one gets rabid after a while. You begin wishing you were a mad dog. You want to go out and get your teeth around those bastards. Drive them over a cliff. What matter if a few of the innocent go along with them? When it gets to that point then you know that you've become heathen yourself."

He sat shivering beside me on the bed. His nose dripped. He wept. I patted his shoulder. I tucked my two hands up around his cheeks.

"I'm sorry, Richard," I said. "I take it back. You're the dearest person in my life. I believe in you."

"You can't take it back. Don't even bother. I just thought you'd understand."

"I do. I really do."

"Nonsense. No you don't. Very few people do. It's too much to expect that they would. But you know what? That doesn't change anything. It changes nothing. Because this is how it's going to be. Long after my life is over and after yours is over — after everybody we know is dead and any children who are this minute being born are long since dead — long, long after all that is past there is going to come a time when the heathens are going to be no more. Wiped out, sopped up, or transformed. They are going to have fled or will have been changed by people like me. Yes, laugh if you want to, but it's the truth. I'd stake my life on it. We are not so few in number, you know. There are millions like us. And when people see us coming, see us in action, they are going to run. Sure, the heathens will put up a fight, but without knowing it they are going to be retreating all the time. They are going to retreat off the face of the earth. In *full* retreat, one of these days. You may think it's the other way around. My files would certainly indicate this appears to be the case. But there are things, people, incidents, happenings, *movements* not recorded there. Full-scale dynamite *rebellions!* Don't blink. Don't sit on your hands, fluttering your eyes at me. I'm talking about *waves and waves*, rearguard *campaigns*, underground *works*! About heathens besieged. I say fuck your missiles. Fuck your bombs. Fuck your radiation. Gloom's all right, but fuck despair. Sure, go at the bastards, pin their knuckles to the walls, but there is a bigger movement afoot that will make the button-pushers go more than blind. They will be screaming for mercy. You know what it is, this *movement*, this *tide*? Well, you're too stupid, Suzy, to know. You want to see movies, you want to jump rope, play hopscotch, sit back and scratch your head. I'll give you a year or two. Right now you've got a strong dose of heathenism in your bones, you're a *latent* heathen, one in the masses, the great wash of ordinary people, from the Greek *maza*, meaning you're just short of barley cake. But I don't count you out. You got a certain glimmer in your eye. But this is deceptive stuff, this movement I was talking about. I'd wager those sons of bitches are retreating even now. I can't prove it, not many would agree with me, but I think they are. Do you understand? Do you have any idea what I'm rattling on about? This, goddamnit: long, long, *long* after all of us are dead, yes, but not so long or far off I can't smell it. The time is coming. Billions of people, all sorts, are out there this minute leading the charge."

The next morning after John Yanks left both my parents knocked on my door. They'd been knocking since God knows when, unable to get in because of the chair I'd propped under the doorknob. All I could see of them were their noses.

"Child?" they said. "Suzy, now don't you panic!"

I lugged my head up off the hot pillow. I'd had a wonderful sleep. I'd been figuring I'd maybe put in a special heavy-duty day that day and do something really interesting as I sat at my mirror turning strands of hair around my finger. Go through a magazine or two, write my name in the dust... maybe open the curtains and spend a long while just staring out of the window. The house next door is kind of patchy; you can see four or five different paint colors and the gutter has thick moss in it. There's a little tree out there where the neighbors used to tie their dog. Woof, he was called. But I must have been quite little when this happened. I haven't seen those people or that dog in nine or ten years.

"Honey, open the door," my dad said. "Let us in."

I got the chair pulled away. I fell back into bed.

"Honey, we have big news for you," he said.

"Yes," clapped my mother. "Your father has found you a job. It will be interesting. You'll love it."

They beamed at me. Mother was at my closet, swinging hangers back. Father was sitting on my bed. He had my hand in his. He began kissing my fingers.

"Give it a try," he whispered. "That's all I ask. That you take a swing at it."

I smiled at him. He was so very nice when he wanted to be.

"I'm too tired," I said. "I was thinking I'd spend the whole day in bed."

"There!" mother said. "Didn't I tell you?"

"Hold on, mother," daddy said. "Stay calm, why don't you?"

"Calm!" she muttered. "In this hell-hole?"

"Get up, darling," father said. He let go of my hand and pulled the covers back. Then he pulled them up again because I was naked.

Mother flung a dress out at me. "It's high time this nonsense ended," she cried. "The next thing we'll be hearing is that it's our fault she's acting this way."

"Do it, honey," father said. "Try. Do it for me, if not for yourself. John Yanks is expecting you. You'll have a fine time, don't you worry. And if you don't like it, well then, you can quit. No questions asked."

"That's her trouble," said mother. "You've always pampered her. She'd have stood on her own two feet from the start, without you around."

His face got red. I thought he'd lash back at her and they'd scream and yell and go on about their own business, forgetting about me. I hoped they would. But he patted my cheek and smiled and moved to the door.

"Mom will help you dress," he said. "She'll make you look pretty. I'll go start us a hefty breakfast. You'll need it, now you're a working girl."

Mother went silent as he left the room. She stared at me, shaking her head.

I sat drooped over the edge of the bed, my arms down between my legs. My breasts had tiny creases in them. My nipples were flat, like something that hadn't quite made it to the top of their sandpiles. They were the same dreary color as the rest of me.

"Sometimes I wonder if you're really my daughter," she moaned. "How'd I come to have you? Put your undies on. I wish for once you'd be sensible and wear a nightie in bed. Your father doesn't want to see you, if that's what you're thinking. Go wash your face. Oh, Suzy, can't you look alive?"

I waited for the water to run warm. I sat on the toilet looking at my splayed feet while it ran. Mother was talking the whole time.

"This print, I think" she said. "That way, if something splatters it won't be so noticeable. Hurry up in there."

Father was in the kitchen, calling. "Hurry up," he said. "I've got toast, coffee...anybody want an egg?"

Mother came into the washroom — the *bath*, I don't know why I can't call it that. The toothbrush room, because that's what I was slowly doing. Scrape, scrape...the yellow would never come off and I didn't care. She sat down on the toilet seat, wiping her eyes. She sounded mournful, like a baleful phantom speaking from deep holes. "I don't know why I'm so wretched," she said. "I can't make your life be anything other than what you want it to be." She sniffed, grabbing at the toilet paper. "So maybe you don't respect me," she said. "What else is new?" She lifted herself up, flushed the toilet, and sat down again. "I love you, Suzy," she said. She bent over and groaned. "This bathroom used to flood all the time," she said. "I tried to flush your nappies away." She stood up, still wet-eyed, smoothing her skirt. Her eyes caught mine in the mirror. I looked away only an instant before she did. "When I was a youth I had such ideas," she said. "No matter what your youth, whatever it is, you have them. I met a man from Africa last week. If you are in Africa, suffering the longest drought in history and your stomach is rubbing your backside, you still have them." She stopped crying, dried her eyes with tissue, and moved to the door. "Can't you hurry?" she said. "Do you have to take all year brushing your stupid teeth? Can't you get a little rhythm into your arm? Can't you hear your father calling us?"

"Ready, it's ready!" we heard him call. "It's getting cold."

"I laid out a dress on your bed," she said. "Wear what you want, I don't care."

I sat at the table with the dry toast in one hand, my other around a glass. I was almost dozing. I didn't want breakfast so early. I hardly ever ate with them in the house.

"May I have an apple?" I said.

Mother reached with her own napkin to pat my chin.

"Like a baby," she said. "Where this child needs to be is in an old-folks' home. You're insane if you think this job's going to pan out."

"Yanks is patient," he said. "He'll give her every chance."

"Sure he will," said mother. "I hope you know why it is he's doing this."

"Sure I do. He owes me a favor."

"Favor, nothing," she said. "John Yanks has other ideas."

"About Suzy? You're kidding."

"I wasn't thinking of Suzy."

Father asked her what she meant. He persisted, but she wouldn't say. She only smiled at him, looking coy, hinting that

John Yanks, if he wanted to know, had an interest in her. But father didn't get it; he never did.

"Okay," he told me in the car. "Buckle up. Don't want you going through the windshield on your first day of work." I sat there. Finally he reached over and snapped the belt in place. "The first day of the rest of your life," he said. "Be safe, not sorry." Mother sat unsmiling in the back, making grumpity sounds.

"What is it, Coolie?" he asked her.

"I don't know why I have to sit back here. It seems to me a wife's place would be up front beside her husband. But don't mind me. Nobody in this family ever did."

"You can drive if you want to."

"Oh yes!" she said. "I could have got a cab, too. I could have called for a limousine. I could have asked Princess Grace of Monaco and she would have picked me up."

The princess has died. It said so in one of Richard's magazines.

"Hold your head up, honey," she told me. "It isn't the end of the race."

I was thinking of my goldfish. I couldn't remember when I last had fed them, whether yesterday or last week. I was so busy, it seemed to me, I couldn't keep up. I had a few addresses I wanted to write to. I wanted to go back and look at my fish.

"Relax, Suzy," my dad said. "It's no great ordeal. Believe me, you're up to this."

"I've always hated backseats," mother said. "I was always stuffed into backseats when I was a child. A hundred elbows were ever poking into me."

"Come up here," said dad. "Sit in my lap."

She didn't speak any more. I dozed. Father dropped her off where she worked — ("Here you are. Picayune Enterprises. Good-bye, dear." Picayune. They made car seats for little kids. They made plastic bed-a-bye rests, very nice, and backpacks for parents on the go) — and then drove me into this big empty parking lot where there was a bakery, a restaurant, and a filling station. There was a supermarket. He drove across the white lines and all the way around to the back.

"Come on, honey," he said. "Now don't you chicken out on me." He pushed me up a ramp toward this back door which said "Do Not Enter." "Try to smile," he said. He knocked and the door was opened for him. He greeted a man or two and went on through the stockroom, heading for the bright lights at the front. "Hair in your mouth," he said, brushing it away. "We must cut that, one of these days. Longer than my mother's was." There were stacks and stacks of apples around, and lots of cabbages and lettuces. I stopped by the apples, but he came back for me. He put back the one I had in my hand, and waved his own hands in front of my face. "This little piggy went to market," he said. "Wake up. Today is a new day. Today things begin to happen to you."

"I'm so sleepy," I said.

"Ah, Suzy!" he said.

There were about one million empty drink bottles around; he pushed me by these. He guided me along to a little office near the front. It had John Yanks's name in green letters on the glass. "John Yanks, Mgr.," it said.

But John Yanks wasn't in. He told me to stand there while he went to find him. "Now don't fade on me," he said. "One day you're going to thank your lucky stars I did this for you. You're going to want to kiss my feet a thousand times.

"Don't cry," he said.

But I did. My eyes were wet and I only wished I could curl up somewhere. I wished I had left my room when they had asked me to; I wished I had made friends and gone out into the neighborhood and been like everyone else. Then they wouldn't have made me come here and cause all this trouble for John Yanks. I didn't mind John Yanks, I was sure John Yanks would turn out to be a very nice man; but I wished I were back in my little room, going on with my life, being happy with myself.

"Did you explain it to her?" John Yanks said. He and my father were coming toward me, John Yanks looking me over... shaking my hand. John Yanks had on a gray suit, as did my father, but they didn't look remotely alike. My father was much shorter and quite a bit older and looked a lot more worried. He looked shabby beside John Yanks. "I'm totally confident everything will go well," John Yanks told me. "I know you're going to be worth your weight in gold."

"I didn't get around to the job description," father said. "Be best if you went through it with her."

"Sure," John Yanks said. "You run along. I'll look after things from here."

My father gave me a kiss and whispered in my ear: "Be friendly," he said. Then he went off. He didn't want to go, I could tell.

"Well now!" John Yanks said, stepping back to take a good look at me. "What a pretty dress! Makes you look fifty years old!" He laughed and took my hand. He led me around the store, introducing me to the butcher and the produce manager, the stock boys and the checkout girls. He didn't seem to notice or mind that he had to keep waiting for me. I saw a few strange looks go around when I didn't speak up. I'd mumble and they'd lean forward and say, "What was that? Pardon? Didn't catch it?" — and John Yanks would laugh and say, "Suzy. She said her name was Suzy. Suzy's going to put hustle into this place."

"Suzy Q.," they said. "Welcome aboard, Suzy Q."

"Need any help, say the word."

"Hi, Suzy. What nice long hair."

Such a lot of stuff like that they said. I was sleepy, feeling dreamy, but they were all so friendly I didn't mind being in the store a bit. I wondered if something wasn't happening to me.

John Yanks led me to the rear, by the cheeses and cold cuts. There was a little booth there with flags, and a little counter with a fry pan on it. "JOHN YANKS FINEST DELI," the sign said. "SAMPLE ME."

"Stay here," he said. "Be back in a minute."

He disappeared and for about half an hour I was alone. I scrunched up my shoulders and stood behind the counter much of the time. There were white paper plates and about a thousand paper napkins. There was a bucket filled with toothpicks. A stool was lodged down under the counter and I brought it out and sat on it. I rested my head on my hands; it wasn't so different from being in my room.

One of the checkout girls showed up, the brown-haired one, in her arms rolls and rolls of salamis and sausages and weiners and such. "Here they are," she said. "Mr. Yanks said I should go through the routine."

She said I was to fry up dainty tidbits, cut very small, and put toothpicks into them, and serve them to customers on little crackers. I was to keep saying how delicious everything was and how much it cost. I should keep crackers out on a plate, never too many. "Wait here," she said, "I'll get the crackers. You don't say much, do you?"

But it was a stock boy who brought the crackers. "We had another lady last week," he said, "but she quit. Said she was getting fat." He stacked the crackers and went away. One or two customers were already strolling the aisles, pushing their carts. They looked at the sign and looked at me, and went on by, looking unsure. I had to go to the washroom and wished someone had told me where it was. The aisles filled and carts went by me every which way. I sliced a sausage and got the slices in the pan with their toothpicks but the pan didn't heat up. There was a mustard jar but I couldn't get it open.

A lady in a knit suit with two children riding in her cart was watching me. "You have to plug it in," she said. "There must be an electrical cord somewhere." She came behind the booth and crawled around a while on her knees. "Here it is," she said. She plugged it in. "The red light should come on," she said. "Why isn't it working?" She looked around. "Keep an eye on my boys," she said. She disappeared, following the black cord to where it was leading.

"What's your name?" one of the boys asked. "I'm four years old," he said. "He's only two. He's my brother. We're the Williamses."

The red light came on on the fryer.

"Our mother was a nun," the boy said.

The lady came back. She was smiling. She had black hair and eyes so alive they were like flowers. "It wasn't plugged in at that end," she said. She got her purse from the cart and began searching through it. "Now where is it?" she said.

The larger boy studied her, then turned and swatted his brother. The swatted one started crying. "Oh listen to him," said the woman. But she kept on searching. "Good. Here it is." She passed a sheet of yellow paper to me. "MEETING TONIGHT," it said, "AT INTERNATIONAL HOUSE. Death squads continue to kill innocent peoples in El Salvadore."

"Come if you can," she said. She told the boys to wave good-bye.

"I enjoyed talking to you," the older one said. "We're having noodles for dinner."

I looked away from their retreating figures to find a man staring straight at me. He was wearing Levis and a frilly shirt. A beige jacket was hooked over his shoulder. "Here, now," he said. "What's this?" He reminded me of Richard because of how he stood with his legs spread, his arms folded. He never stopped looking into my eyes.

"Smells good," he said. "May I partake?"

He picked up a plate containing all of the little sausage morsels. He dabbed mustard on the plate and, one by one, plucked the sausages into his mouth. He ate about fourteen.

"Hold on a minute," he said. He disappeared down one of the aisles and stayed lost for some time; then I saw him over in the eggs section. He came back. He had two brown eggs and a small jar of Dijon mustard. "Fry these up," he said, placing the eggs in my hand. "Wait. You'll need butter." He went away again, returning with a stick of Land o' Lakes. "Be generous with it," he said. "Fry one up for yourself. You don't have any coffee back here, do you? Hold on. Take no action until my return."

He was gone for about three minutes. He came back with two coffees in Styrofoam cups. "I hope you take it black," he said. "Nothing wrong with black. Throw on more sausage. Sprinkle of oregano wouldn't hurt. Float a slice of salami over that egg.

"Chew," he said, once we were eating. "Succulent. Keeps a body fit. Nice deli John Yanks has here."

Others loitering nearby he shooed away.

"Closed for business," he told them. "We got a few more kinks to work out."

John Yanks came by. "Christ, that smells good," he said. "Fry me up one."

I did it and he ate it and went away.

"One in a million, that John Yanks," my new friend said. "Like a long lost brother he is. What's your name?"

Suzy, I said.

"What?"

"Suzy."

"Suzy. What a pretty name. You look like a Suzy. Now guess mine."

I can't.

"What?"

"I said, 'I can't.'"

"Good. I thought my hearing had gone. Now listen, Suzy. I'm here to tell you, the two of us are going to get along. How about lunch with me?"

I nodded.

"How about dinner?"

I went on nodding.

"You got the right attitude," he said. "The two of us are going to be something special. What do you say we get out of here? What do you say we go have ourselves a walk in the woods?"

I backed up. He had come behind the counter and was unplugging my fry pan. He wedged a full salami under his arm. He thrust a box of crackers at me. "Sure, a walk," he said. "Nice idea. Woods or beach or the old sidewalk, what do you say? Mostly it's sidewalk around here. But it's your choice. Later, this evening, my place, I'll cook us up a meal. Sound all right? When the cows come home, then you can go, if you've a mind to. If not, then stay. We've got something really special cooking here and I can feel it. Can you?"

Maybe, I said.

"What?"

"Maybe," I said.

"You've got other plans?"

"There's a meeting tonight," I said. "El Salvadore."

I showed him the paper.

"Good," he said. "We'll both go."

I walked briskly with him out through the front door. John Yanks saw me going, and waved.

"One in a million," said my friend. Outside, he stopped me. "Slow down," he said. "How about this? How about we lay out on the beach, get us some sun. Bottle of wine, maybe, if we work up a thirst. You know, when I walked out this morning I had a feeling this was going to happen to me. I felt it in my bones. 'Today's your day, handsome,' I told myself. 'Your luck is taking a turn for the better. Now yesterday this wouldn't have happened. Yesterday I wouldn't have stood a chance. How about you? Was it like that with you?

"Yes," I said. "Yesterday I couldn't have lifted a finger. Yesterday the ants could have hauled me off."

"Same here," he said. He stopped again. "Hold it," he said. "Let's stake out our borders. Let's seal this business right here. No tooting around, where our futures are concerned. I've been by myself too long. Down in a dark hole. If you're not agreeing with me, let's hear it. Avoid all misunderstandings. What I'm saying is I'm feeling this is for keeps. I'm figuring we've found each other. Am I right?"

I took his hand. I led him up the street to the bus stop.

"First I've got to go home," I said. "I've got to feed my fish."

"Fish. All right."

"I've got to change out of this dress."

"How about that! I wasn't going to say so, but that is one awful dress."

The bus came. We got on it.

"I'll show you my room," I said. "I'll show you where I've been living."

"No problem. My time is your time. I'm not letting you out of my sight. We'll feed your fish, change your dress, see your room, then we're off to the races. We're off into real life. Do I have the right idea?"

"I want to take you by Richard's house. I want to tell you all about Richard."

"Fine. I'm sure Richard is a champ."

"He was. Richard was wonderful. He had a lot to say about heathens. He figured one day they'd be no more. That they'd be gone up in smoke."

"Heathens. That I can dig."

"He was keen on this radio lady from Sioux City. 'Hello, heathens!' she'd say. 'Are you with me or against me? Stand up and be counted!' she'd say."

"Sioux City. Rings a bell."

"One day something happened to Richard. We were sitting in this movie house when suddenly he swatted me on the shoulder and said he was fed up with the heathen life. He walked out. I was so engrossed in the movie I let him go. That was the last I saw of him. Now I can't remember what movie it was. Richard disappeared. He dropped off the face of this earth.''

''We can find him. If he's to be found, we can find him. There's just one thing. Why are we riding this bus? My little moped is back there at the supermarket, filled with gas.''

I pulled the cord. At the next stop we got off. We walked along, holding hands.

''No more heathens,'' he said. ''Heathens of all assorted types. I like that idea.''

Then we were running, pulling each other along. Chins up, elbows pumping. Hearts stretching to burst.

''We're fast,'' he said. ''By God, we can run!''

We could. We could really stir up a breeze. We'd be out in the future in no time, I thought. We'd be with Richard, leading the charge.

The Woman's Guide to Home Companionship

WHAT FOLLOWS IS not in my own hand. What follows is being delivered through the good graces of my friend and neighbor Mrs. Vee Beaverdeck of 101 Menzies, who is doing so without cost or complaint. She will aver, if asked, that this is the truth and the whole truth as I know it and that this story or tale is told firsthand and in a calm manner while we are here in my kitchen drinking our two coffees with now and then an ounce of something fortifying on the side.

It is 2:00 A.M. after what I'd call without exaggeration the roughest night of our lives.

We have been sitting around for hours since it happened, trying to figure out how we hooked up with such undesirables in the first place.

Vee says yes, that is the Lord's truth.

I shall now describe Mrs. Vee Beaverdeck to the degree I am able, so that there shall be no mistaking her for another person or persons and in order to assist the authorities. Vee is forty-six years old, two full years and three full months older than I am, though I think I can guarantee she has never acted funny about it. She is close to my own height and with a disposition similar to mine and on the issue of slenderness we both come in with identical high marks, though this was not always the case.

Why, you ask.

Since June I have shed eighteen pounds, all in the strategic places and without experiencing any undue psychological turmoil. Indeed, it was not because of psychological turmoil or unwholesome self-image in the first place that I embarked upon my physical-improvement program. It was a question of being Fulfilled or not being Fulfilled, as the expert told us. I have always been something of a compulsive snacker and the pounds seem to go right on me, right where they shouldn't, so from time to time my span-image of myself is such that without undue duress I engage in a crash program to eliminate all excess flabbiness, though that is hardly the word.

Mrs. Beaverdeck on the other hand has always been of the slim variety, though not so slim you could thread her through a needle, which has been her great good fortune down through the ages and which I think she will admit (she is nodding) she at times feels a little vain about.

I should intrude here to say Mrs. Beaverdeck keeps trying to interrupt me and change what I am saying, but I am not allowing this because it was the agreement we struck before we started out on this dictation. "You will get your turn," I keep telling her, "after I am done." I should explain too the employment of quotations in the previous sentence was because it was a direct quote or ultimatum delivered to Mrs. Vee Beaverdeck one second ago. I hope I will not have to use this technique hereafter, because it is most distracting to find yourself constantly interrupted and corrected and your every word questioned.

Back to the description.

Suffice it to say I took the aerobic course at Fitness Works Incorporated, 427 Fort Street with free parking, and dropped eighteen pounds, the first being always the hardest, as you know. Mrs. Beaverdeck only lost four, whereupon the expert let her know she need not lose any additional poundage. Be that as it may, I got my muscles toned and my stomach flat and now look smarter than I ever have, whereas Mrs. Vee Beaverdeck has since time immemorial been able to wear whatever she has wanted to wear without thinking twice about it. Now we wear the same size dress, with my feet maybe a half-size larger depending on the make, and double A whereas she's single A.

She paints her toes and I do not.

I am this minute wearing a house robe which belonged to her but which she gave to me because it looked so much better on me thanks to the color of my eyes, which it picks up and highlights, together with my hair.

My bones are bigger so I think I still look larger and more cumbersome, though she claims this is my own personal delusion and little hang-up.

It is time we paused now to refreshen our drinks and sort out in a private and unpublicized manner the issue raised above, since as Vee says this is not a subject totally pertinent to this document and anyhow we have both got to stop crying.

We have got to face up, Vee says, to the consequences of what we have done.

Hi, we are now back, and Vee has sworn that she will take my dictation properly and not in any way undermine my account of our activities this awful evening.

To pick up where we left off:

I definitely have more bosom and we have agreed that this is why I feel larger than Mrs. Beaverdeck, when the truth is that for all practical purposes our bodies are identical. Mrs. Beaverdeck's breasts are sweet and certainly ample, if a little catty-cornered. On this score I feel the nod goes to her whatever the case, the reason being she is more in the Movement than I am and hence does not wear brassieres, which gives her a pronounced if unfair edge on the stares-and-whistles front, that being proved each time the two of us step out shopping. Let me insert also the news that while Mrs. Beaverdeck and I have numerous areas of conflict, on such matters for instance as the wearing of brassieres, we are in shining agreement on the abortion issue, women in the priesthood, on how ninety percent of the world's husbands stack up, etcetera or for instance the politics of certain warmongering nations which shall remain nameless.

Vee is this minute dressed in a black chiffon gown bought from Coordinates Yes!, a stylish store in the heart of town which we both frequent and not too expensive though occasionally their manners could be improved. She has a striped black-and-white silk scarf around her throat, and sheer knee-high hose of midnight blue, with a pair of old Capezzio shoes on her feet because of how she came running out of her house so fast tonight she was practically hysterical. She has long black hair which is now pinned up to her head, along the sides anyway. I have more gray in mine, sorry to say, though it hardly ever shows because of a certain high-quality if expensive rinse which I will swear by. Funny enough, my skin is darker than Vee's with her black hair, despite my being in the blond spectrum thanks to my devoted parents who were both good Christians and will never again be able to hold up their heads once the newspapers get hold of this dictated confession. Vee's skin is definitely on the pale or albinic side, since she has not had more than an instant's sunshine strike her lovely figure since she was a child at Ocean View, which I understand is a beach-front-and-carnival type place outside Norfolk, Virginia. It is pretty bold and striking, if you've ever seen Vee — that contrast between black which is her favorite color and her black hair with her dazzling white skin which does not have a blemish on it that I've ever seen.

Pardon. Mrs. Vee announces she has a cute birthmark the size of a dime on her left inner thigh next to what she calls her "chief asset."

As for yours truly I do not have any marks or disfigurations over the whole of my flesh save those administered in recent times by my objectionable husband.

Mrs. Vee Beaverdeck interrupts to say that I should say up

there where she spoke of her most cherished parts she was speaking "in the ironical."

The subject's eyes are her best features. They are very large and entrancing, with naturally long lashes, plus she has a lively animated face, as I do myself, and more especially tonight as we sit here pouring ourselves coffee and spirits, which we are in part doing in order to keep up our spirits and to get done and accomplished the job we have set for ourselves before we close up shop and let come what must come: the terrible shame and our names and likenesses splashed in banner headlines across the nation.

Vee says thanks to God we do not have children, inasmuch as unbearable would be their agony and their lives ruined because what we have done would be a bitter tonic.

Amen.

It may well be that we are having more to drink than is good for us under the circumstances, but let it be known we are of sound mind and strictly responsible for our actions and will not plead self-defense or temporary insanity or any of that stuff that you read about. Nor do we yet anyhow regret anything we have done or see how, given the circumstances and our emotional states and how over these past few months we have been driven to it, how it could have been avoided.

Nor do we intend to shrivel and cry and fall down in a faint when they come for us. Suffice it to say we mean to stand on our own two feet, giving as well as we get. We will go with our two V fingers high, like in the Movement.

Time out.
Time in.

We are back now, Mrs. Vee Beaverdeck with a pillow to soften her behind and a new writing tablet to take down this dictation as I hereby give it, each word the truth as I have always found the truth to be relevant.

Blemish and all, as Vee says.

Vee says that I should remind everyone that since June of the current year, together with our loyal attendance at Fitness Works Incorporated, a going and respectable concern, we have both been running on the shoulders of our noted highway one half-hour each morning and another half-hour around sunset and that we are now up to four and five miles without hassle or undue sudation. In fact, what we have noticed is that gentlemen of the male persuasion are frequently pitched into unseemly fits of passion by no more than the thin sheen of sweat over our jogging bodies, with the result that they often swerve off the road or beep their horns or sometimes even execute daredevil U turns and return to embark upon the most boring and impossible advances two women at our stage of enlightenment could conceivably imagine.

Whereas we could take or leave this behavior, our abominable husbands have, from the beginning, pitched a gasket. We have taken immeasurable abuse, alternating with a certain stonewalling, over our fitness endeavors. Vee remembers that when we first went out on runs her husband would sit drinking his beer in front of the TV and laughing at her for (quote) "thinking you are some kind of female athelete."

What my own husband said, his chapter-one remark, was (quote), "What I wonder is what kind of effect all this exercising is going to have on your little red fire engine." Little red fire engine is my husband's he thinks quaint euphemism for my sexual parts. If the reader finds this sinister and distasteful and bespeaking of deep dark problems with his sexual attitudes then I am with that reader to the nth degree.

It is with a heavy heart that I utilize material of this X-rated type but accuracy dictates it and leaves me no choice.

Mind you, this was way back in June when there was still some semblance of sanity at 101 and 137 Menzies.

Vee says that I should take off the kid gloves and give a few more sterling examples of their truly rotten behavior.

But I believe I can trust the reader to already understand what kind of "gentlemen" we have here.

Also, it is not my hope to give a full and documented account of their crimes against us and nature, for that would take a book and lots more time than I am willing to give to those two throwbacks.

Let it be known, in any event, that we have spotless reputations in this town and no one to our knowledge, among those with whom we carry on a daily business, has ever had occasion to say word one against us nor have we been involved in any previous criminal wrongdoing.

Hold on a minute. Vee has gone and got my Polaroid and I have taken and labeled three pictures depicting her cut and bruised face, as well as two of the back porch and door which shows what a rage my own husband was in earlier in the evening when he left this place.

Vee or Mrs. Beaverdeck has likewise taken a picture of me in knickers and bra, which shows I am anything but the "slick pig" he has since June been calling me.

Vee has said she can think of a number of men who would be willing to pay a hundred dollars for a copy of the above-named photo. I have said I can think of two or three I'd let have it for free.

We have had us another drink and are presently making a fresh pot of coffee.

We have also looked back over this document and read it aloud, because my friend and neighbor Mrs. Vee Beaverdeck claims I go off on too many tangents, for instance what she looks like.

Vee Beaverdeck is beautiful. She is beautiful and she is my dearest friend and I have threatened to go directly to the authorities and confess our cruel deed if she doesn't put on the page exactly what I dictate to her.

You should understand, however, that many of the comments and asides we make to each other are not being entered into this document, since we feel much of it is not your business to know and for once in our lives we are doing exactly what we want to do.

We shall now have another drink, and as Vee says "screw the coffee."

Mrs. Vee Beaverdeck, I have discovered only this evening, has had business training, and I am proud of her. For six years before her unfortunate marriage she worked for Stan Bask Associates, a well-known investment firm in this city. She advanced in this period from clerk-typist to the position of receptionist-supervisor and customarily took dictation from Stan Bask himself, who twice tried to seduce her and once got her pinned down on the carpet floor in front of his desk.

Suffice it to say that Mrs. Beaverdeck now looks back upon that experience with a very different eye.

She is now back from the phone where she has got Mr. Stan Bask up from a sound sleep and told him exactly what we think of him.

He professes that he "does not remember," and reminds her that "we were both young then."

I have now been subjected to a long speech from Mrs. Vee Beaverdeck on the importance of the Woman's Movement and such questions as, "How can you, Violet Witherspoon, sit quietly by?" I have not heard many of these questions because I have gone to the bathroom. From my seat on the toilet, however, I have reminded Vee Beaverdeck of what we both have tonight done to our husbands.

"You can hardly say, after my actions this evening, that I have sat (quote) quietly by (unquote)."

That is a direct quote.

Vee Beaverdeck, who has admitted she said so out of tipsiness, has apologized for delivering inflammatory accusations against one Violet Witherspoon, domiciled at 137 Menzies.

By common vote we shall now pause, for we are overcome with giggles. Take five.

Back now. The old clock on the wall cries out the time, 3:12 A.M. In this interval have we skulked by devious route and cunning to 101 Menzies, there to "view the remains," to replenish our bar stock, and to secure an overnight bag for Mrs. Vee Beaverdeck, including toothbrush, stockings, underwear, makeup, hair dryer, the outfit she means to wear tomorrow for whatever official inquiries might involve us, together with the book I lent her years ago, inherited from my mother and containing numerous pressed flowers, entitled *The Woman's Guide to Home Companionship*.

We have had a great laugh over this volume, as you can imagine, though it put me in tears to think of my mother eternally slaving away and all for what?

The "remains" remain intact and unchanged. We did not long study the situation, however, for the macabre, as Vee stated, has limited appeal.

I shall now pick up some of the loose ends.

Vee Beaverdeck believes I should not have described her breasts as "catty-cornered." She has bared herself and I have taken a Polaroid and we are now researching the result. I say to Vee, "Your left nipple points to nine o'clock, your right to three o'clock, and I call that catty-cornered."

Vee Beaverdeck spends one half-hour in my bathroom behind locked door studying this matter. Then she calls for her drink, which I pass through. A minute or so later she calls me in. She is seated on the bath edge, crying out her beautiful eyes.

"Vee," I say, "I was only kidding."

"I know," she says.

"I mean it," I say. "It was only a joke."

"I know," she says.

Then Vee Beaverdeck looks at me and with a broken heart says, "I could get a plastic surgeon to make small cuts on the inside of each breast and get them pointed straight."

We then bawl, for it comes to us in the same split second that our men have totally undermined our self-image, and it is almost as if we can hear them laughing.

It is some time before we are able again to stand upright.

This has nothing to do with strong drink, though our glasses stand empty.

Vee says: "I said I was going to get drunk, and I meant it."

So forthwith we pour ourselves another round.

We are both wide awake at 4:00 A.M. and wondering when grief or guilt, or fear or total despair, will set in, but to this hour, along those lines, we feel nothing.

"What will they do to us?"

"I will claim total amnesia."

These statements and others like them have been made and repeated since the perpetration of the very deed itself, though I have decided and Vee has agreed that such disclosures are not to be admitted into this chronicle. Even so.

"Should we get in the car and run?" says Vee.

"Vee," I say, "we have between us exactly twenty-seven dollars and eleven cents."

"Two beautiful women, alone in the dark night, cannot leave a cold trail. It is impossible. At the first gas station or truckstop we come to some man will make a pass at us, we will be compelled to resist his advances, and before we know it five thousand peace officers will be hot on our trail."

I mope. I tell Vee to put it down that I am moping because she has entered the above statement directly onto these pages. "Vee," I say, "I am supposed to be dictating my statement."

"So dictate," she says.

We have a little cry because we have fought with each other.

Vee asks if I meant it back there at the start of this piece when I spoke of her beauty. That interests her, she says, though she can not quite see its point in terms of this document.

"Take this down, Vee," I say. "The point of it was to stress that while our husbands found us objectionable and undesirable, men and in fact anyone with an objective eye would find us quite the opposite." I remind her that I did not kill myself those weeks at Fitness Works Incorporated for nothing, and that we have not run upwards of five thousand miles over the past six months so that our husbands could abuse us and poke fun.

"Also, we were pretty sharp cookies to begin with," I say.

Something in this remark drives Vee to reflect that seventeen men in the past year have propositioned her. Three of them, directly. That is, they put their arms around her and began kissing her and whispering about motels.

I am stunned. Only two have approached me.

"One was your husband," she says.

"Vee, put this in," I say. "I am not surprised."

"He was the one most adamant."

I am not surprised.

"Vee," I say, "are you sure? Seventeen?"

"I could be mistaken about a couple of them," Vee says.

"But it was how they looked at me. I also didn't tell quite the truth about Mr. Stan Bask. The truth is I never knew to what extent I was willing. Alas, he was a handsome devil. So debonair."

We agree it is the debonair gent who most carries the day.

Vee Beaverdeck makes it clear she was never a fallen woman. She wonders whether this was a mistake. She laments that all she wants is a little happiness in her life. "Like," says she, "when jogging."

She says she is getting tired of taking dictay, and is feeling dopey and sentimental and would like to shoot herself.

She goes over to the kitchen faucet and lets cold water stream over her head.

I have gone into my bedroom and poked around in my cedar chest until I've found my husband's old love letters. I look at them a while. I don't know why and certainly I don't care. It strikes me with a jolt that his old letters are wholly illiterate. All he talks about is his job and drinking and the weather and what he'd do if he had me near him, and how dumb everybody is. He writes in a very large hand so he can fill nine or ten pages. He includes little drawings of what sheep do to each other. It is a funny thing to me how I would clutch this trash to my chest in those days and feel absolutely divine and glorious.

It is clear from his letters that he never had a brain in his head and that all was subterfuge from the start.

"He mentions you," I tell Vee. "He says his buddy Carl has taken up with 'a very weird woman who is very odd.'"

Vee says, "Let me see that."

She has now stopped receiving dictation to look it over.

I say: All right, Vee. It is too late to save her from it. She's going to come to that part in the letter where my husband-to-be says that Carl tells him he's pretty sure he's going to get from her what he wants and that he's already had more than a taste of it. "She's hot-to-trot in the old backseat," Carl says. "Guess they just can't resist old Carl's charm."

"I don't want to take any more dictay," Mrs. Vee Beaverdeck has said. So I've dropped down here to do it myself. What I wonder about is why they've treated us the way they have. I don't think they originally set out to become demented. I know they don't think of themselves as mean. We've never mattered to them so they've gone about their lives exactly as they've wanted, never thinking about us except to say what trouble we've caused them. Floppy appendages, I guess we are, like an extra arm that nobody wants. It was not the big things anyway that led us to our mission. It was the little things they did, like how they would look at each other with sick smiles anytime we spoke, and how they pitched their beer cans out of the car window, and scoffed at flowers we brought into the house; it was how they left wet coffee spoons in the sugar bowl and abused our friends and swore up and down Richard Nix was such a great foreign-policy president, not to mention the whole cutthroat heathen gang our other halves aligned themselves with. Etcetera. Etcetera. It was how they looked, too: with their hair combed down over their brows, their ears sticking out, the stupid baseball caps on the back of their heads, and the seats of their pants flopping down to their knees. Mostly it was how you could never get out of them one word of moral support, not one word about their emotional feelings on the private home-front question as it relates to those closest and dearest to them, and if you expected support from those two on your personal dilemmas ranging from A to Z you'd be better off putting in a call to the Ayatollah what's-his-name.

The truth is we did it to them because they never seemed to feel anything. Not even when we did it.

My friend and beloved neighbor Mrs. Vee Beaverdeck is this moment overcome with uncontrollable fatigue and hereby demands that I cease with these memoirs. She declares with a shiver that she has this second had the most terrible thought; to wit, that we have not in point of fact succeeded in dispensing with our husbands, but that throughout the torment of this evening and the subsequent drenching of ourselves with alcohol we have merely been displaying wishful thinking. She urges that we abandon this post immediately and scurry posthaste to view the miserable bodies.

Agreed. A foul thought indeed. Take twenty.

Hi! I'm back.

Nope, we've done it, all right. They are definitely gone from this world. They shall never again take advantage of frail womanhood or sneer at a pile of dirty dishes or behave generally like inhuman scoundrels.

They shall know better next time.

"Let's put pennies over their eyes," Vee Beaverdeck said. "Let's pull the sheets up under their chins. Let's get rid of these beer cans and cigarette butts they've left here and take a Polaroid of them in their glory, in case we again have doubts."

The photo turned out ever so nicely. It seemed to catch mine flinching when the flash went off. It seemed to me I heard both of them groan, but that was only my nerves working overtime.

"Mine, too," said Vee. "I've had it."

She said hers looked nicer than he ever had. "You'd almost

think him human," she said. She pointed out a dimple in his left cheek. "Or is that where I got him with the heel of my shoe?"

We sat out on the back deck measuring the dark houses all around and looking up out of tired relief at the man in the moon.

"It's no man," Vee said. "That's my grandmother."

"She's nice," I said. "She looks like she knows a woman's true place."

Vee Beaverdeck stretched out flat on her back. She sighed about a thousand times.

"This is a one-shot deal," she said. "I'm not cut out for murder and mayhem."

Ditto here. It's too gruesome, if that's any news.

Dirty Heels of the
Fine Young Children

THE REASON MY WIFE left me is she was unfaithful. She was unfaithful to me and to the children and to her own self too. I don't mean in the usual way. I just mean she was unfaithful. She was flighty and loose and spiteful and her children have caught it too.

I say to them, "Your mama was unfaithful" and you ought to see the black looks I get. "She was," I say, "and you know it."

They fly right out the door. There they go, *slam-bang!*

And they don't return, most times, till way after midnight. Which makes me feel like a fool, standing out in my yard calling in my shrillest voice:

"Agnes, you come home!"

"Sarah, you come home!"

"Monkey, you get your little bottom in this house this instant and I don't mean maybe!"

Frankly, I feel stupid and more than a little uncomfortable out there night after night yelling for them, knowing Agnes and Sarah and poor little Monkey who is only three are not even listening, though everyone else is. I know what my neighbors are saying:

"Oops, looks like they've run off too, just like their mama did. Looks like they've gone lickety-split too."

"You can't blame them," I hear people saying.

I even hear people laughing sometimes, and once in a while old Jim Broom from next door will poke his ugly head over the fence to tell me to lower the volume, I'm scaring his cats.

His *cats,* that's right, that's what he's always saying.

People see another person having a run of bad luck, they just can't help taking it as a joke, because they're so glad the bad luck isn't theirs.

I don't even speak to Jim Broom. I keep on calling the children. It's way past dark and they haven't done their schoolwork or had dinner or washed up, and anything could happen to them out there.

That's one of the things their mama didn't think about, I guess, how they'd be running wild. It's what I mean about her being unfaithful. She ought to have known.

The truth is I sometimes wished they would run away and never come back because (one) in many ways they are just like her and (two) they've got her same mean streak and (three) it isn't easy looking after three hellcats by your own self and (four) if they did I might be able to think about my own life once in a while.

But a father has got to do the job. If a father didn't, in my situation, who would?

Take that mean streak: here I am thinking primarily of the oldest, Agnes, because hers is most pronounced. How she learned it I don't know, because the little demon is only ten. Every day she comes home from school and says:

"I saw mama at the store today."

or

"Mama was in talking to my principal today."

or

"I saw mama last night in the park eating popcorn with her new boyfriend."

or

"Mama said you ought to do something about Sarah's hair."

or

"Mama says we all ought to have more spending money."
or
"Mama says we can stay out as late as we want to any night we want to."
or
"Mama says you sound like a fool with all that yelling."

Why does she do it? She does it (one) because each time my eyes pop out at the thought that their mama *could* be back in town and (two) because Agnes has been so hurt by her mama's running off that she *has* to make up these stories and (three) because she has her mama's mean streak and ought to be taken over my lap and whipped until her spirit is broken and she confesses that all this stuff she thinks to tell me is total hogwash.

Such had been my thinking until last night. Last night, it seems to me, all this meanness came to a head, and now I'm beginning to see our business more clearly. I've beamed in on what's been going on around here.

Here's how it happened. One, they'd been out all evening, not answering to nothing. Two, when the three of them tried slipping in around midnight on tiptoe I jumped out from my hiding place in the front-hall closet and I caught all three by their hair and their coats and shook the daylights out of them.

Agnes piped up and said: "You better stop that because mama says we can have you put in jail. She says you are not allowed to brutalize children any more and if you don't believe me you can run right over to Mrs. Tucker's place and ask her because that's where mama is."

Well I stopped shaking them. One, I was winded and, two, she *could* have been over at Mrs. Tucker's place because that Tucker woman was as bad as their mama was and the two of them had been like twins.

"What's this?" I said. "You're telling me your mama is over at that Tucker house?"

"Why would I lie?" said Agnes. "I got no reason to lie about a thing like that. Mama's been over there for a week. She says she might stay permanently at Mrs. Tucker's place and we can come see her any time."

Now *this* I thought was strange, because Tucker's only got two little rooms and she's got this man living with her, Joe Espozita.

"Yeah?" I said. "Where does your mama sleep?"

"On a pallet in the kitchen," Agnes said. "She's getting in a foam mattress tomorrow. And anyway Joe's almost never there because he works nights. So there's plenty of room. Mama says it's a very pleasant arrangement."

"And cheap too," Sarah pops up, "which mama needs, because she says you have cut off all her money."

Now that convinced me. Because any time Sarah tells a lie she starts blushing, and she didn't blush when she said that. And I also knew Joe drove taxi most nights. But still I knew how sharp these children could be, so I pushed Little Monkey back into the corner by the coats and I asked her:

"Are they telling the truth?"

"Yes."

"You saw your mama tonight?"

"Yes."

"Was she at Tucker's?"

"Yes."

"She's living there?"

"Yes."

"On a pallet in the kitchen?"

"Yes."

But she hesitated on that last one, so I got a good grip on her shoulder and pressed her back even harder.

"Yes?"

"Well tomorrow she's getting foam."

The other two were tugging at my sleeve, trying to get me

away from Little Monkey. Each time Monkey said yes they'd been adding their own little chorus: "See! See! Now do you believe us?"

"What does this Joe character look like?" I asked Monkey.

She looked lost for a minute. I noticed her eyes roaming over to her sisters for help.

"I don't know," she finally said. "He drives his taxi most nights."

That did it. I knew they'd been over to the Tucker woman's place and that they'd seen their mama. I began to think that maybe they'd been seeing her every night.

Which sure wasn't being faithful to me.

"All right," I said, "I am going to see about this. You little kids go wash your faces now and get straight to bed."

"Why?" said Agnes. "It's hardly even after midnight."

"What about our dinner?" said Sarah.

"Just do it," I said, "and no back talk from any of you."

They grumbled but they did it. All three of them trooped together into the bathroom and they washed their faces together over the sink, whispering madly the whole time.

"Stop that whispering," I said. "What new meanness are the three of you plotting now?"

Agnes popped up: "Mama says we ought to be made to take whole baths sometime. She says we stink."

I saw purple. It was all I could do to keep from swatting the three little devils hard as I could.

"If your mama thinks she can take care of you any better than I can then she's welcome to try. If she wants to come home and make you take baths she's welcome to try that too. Lord knows I can't. I can't even find you. Every day I remind you to take your baths but no you're off streaking through the neighborhood, disappearing, paying no attention to nobody, and piling home after midnight when you should have been home in bed for hours."

"That's what mama says," Agnes said. "She says we need discipline. She says it's against the law how you let us do."

That time I really did smack out. I smacked out hard, but all three ducked and went around me or between my legs and went on scrambling every which way.

"That's it!" Agnes screeched. "Mama says you don't know how to control your emotions, which is why she left you in the first place. She says you are like a child. She says you are a mean, mean man."

She was down under the bed where I couldn't reach her.

Monkey was off somewhere crying.

Sarah was shooting first one place then another.

"Mama says you ought to be committed!" Agnes screeched.

Well I caught her and I was laying into her when Sarah came up behind me and got me over the head with a broom.

"You better not hurt her!" Sarah said.

"You better not!" said Monkey.

But I kept laying into her.

Agnes brought her teeth down on my hand.

"You let go and I'll let go," I said.

She let go but only to screech, "You leave us alone! Mama says you ain't even our daddy!"

That really got to me. I drifted back to my room in a daze, trying to figure how their mama could ever have sunk so low as to tell them that.

I figured it up, sitting on my bed.

It just wasn't the truth; I *had* to be their daddy.

I could hear them in their room, plotting and whimpering and whispering.

After a while I started getting mad. I took off my pajamas and put on my everyday clothes and put on my hat. I'd decided I was going over to that Tucker woman's house and really have it out with their mama. I was going to go at her with both barrels. I was going to prove to her how unfaithful and unfit for living she was, and let her know that if she ever came near my children again I was going to find myself a gun and shoot her.

Well who is it drives up in the taxi but Joe Espozita.

"Kinda late to be going out, isn't it?" he says to me.

I mumble something. For some reason I have always been embarrassed being in his company and any time I have to take a taxi somewhere I've always made sure I didn't get his. But tonight in all the confusion I hadn't remembered.

"Climb in then," he said.

So I climbed in. But I wasn't about to let him know I was going over to his house, so I said, "Take me downtown."

"Where downtown?"

"Any place downtown."

He gave me a funny look but finally said, "Okay with me." And drove off.

I could see Agnes and Sarah and little Monkey with their faces plastered against the windows. Damned if they didn't seem to be smiling.

On the way downtown I thought I'd try to get something out of Joe without his knowing.

"How're things over at your house, Joe?" I said.

"So-so."

"And the wife, how's she?"

"So-so, I guess. She don't complain much."

"Must be pretty crowded for you in that place."

"Pretty crowded," he said. "Still, we've got used to it."

"I heard the wife was thinking about having a baby."

"No. No, nothing like that. We're waiting a bit."

"Of course if you had a baby you'd probably have to move. No way three people could live in that small place."

"Oh, I don't know," he said. "A person can make do with pretty near anything."

"That's right," I said. "I guess you could rig up some sort of sleeping arrangement in the kitchen."

"Maybe," he said. "Maybe. Anyway, her and me are waiting a bit."

I asked a few more questions of the leading type, but he wasn't exactly responsive. He wasn't letting anything out. But I got the distinct impression he had some third party staying over at his house and that this went right along with what my children had been saying.

The minute he dropped me off, down by the bus depot, I hailed another taxi and told the driver where I wanted to go.

"Ain't that Joe's address?" he said. "Didn't I just see Joe dropping you off?"

I stayed quiet. There are times when I *hate* this town.

Anyway, he dropped me off.

"Want me to wait?" he said.

Now that was a tough one. Joe lived hell-and-gone from anyplace and I didn't know how I'd get home if the Tucker woman wouldn't let me in. But I couldn't have him hanging around watching because first I had to scout out the place for any sign of my wife.

So what I said was, "How about you come back in one hour?"

"Can't," he said. "I'm going off duty in another minute or two. Had a long hard day."

And before I could figure out a solution he waved his hand and took off.

The children were right. I ought to learn how to drive, and buy us a car.

However, no time now to moan. The Tucker woman's rooms are upstairs over this Chinaman's store. Both the store and the upstairs were shut up tight, no lights anywhere. I was wondering if I could just barge right in when I remembered what my purpose was and how angry I was and that it was my unfaithful wife up there. I paced a bit, boiling over at how she'd told those children I was no daddy of theirs. So after tripping over the garbage cans out back and getting my hat tore off going through rose vines at the side, I strode straight up and knocked fiercely on the door.

"Open up!" I said. "Open up right now!"

It was about ten minutes before a light come on up there, plus about a dozen in the houses all around. One man came out and stood on his porch and stayed there staring at me.

"Are you drunk?" he said.

I turned my back on him.

I heard a window being raised so I stepped back on the walk and saw the Tucker woman poking her head out.

"You!" she said. "My God I haven't seen you in a month of Sundays."

"Well I'm here now," I said.

"Not since Ruthie left you. By God that was the smartest thing she ever done."

"That's why I'm here now," I said. "I've come to see her."

She got this confused look.

"You've come here? You think she's here?"

"I know she's here," I said. "The children told me."

She laughed. I had got her up out of her deep sleep but she wasn't having any trouble laughing.

The man out on the porch went back in. She went on laughing.

"I love those kids," she said. "Those are wonderful kids." And still she laughed.

"Now listen," I said. "You tell my wife to come down here or I'm coming up. I'm having it out with her here tonight or know the reason why."

"God," she said, "you believe it, don't you? You believed those kids. You think she's here."

"Open up," I said.

"You're crazy," she said. "Ruthie isn't anywhere around here. Ruthie's went as far away from you as she could get."

"She's not here, huh?" I said. "Well who is that sleeping on a pallet in your kitchen?"

She started laughing again.

"In my kitchen? Hell, she'd have to be a cat to sleep in my kitchen. There's hardly room to turn around."

Then I remembered her kitchen. It was the size of a matchbox. You couldn't put your foot in that kitchen without tripping over the stove. That's all it was: a stove, a little ice box, and a sink the size of a half dollar.

"Go home," she said. "Take a nerve pill." Then she slapped her brow and got a horrified look: "You've left those children alone!" she said. "You have, haven't you? By God I can't believe it. What kind of father are you? I heard how Agnes and Sarah and Little Monkey been running loose in town night after night. Going unwashed and unfed. Running wild. But I didn't believe it. I simply didn't believe even you could be so negligent."

"I didn't come here to take your abuse," I said.

But I was wilting. I saw I'd made a mistake. Those little wretches had outfoxed me.

"You're going to lose those children," she said. "Welfare is going to come and gobble them up."

I started backing away.

"Okay," I said. "I'm going. But if you hear from that wife of mine you tell her I'm gunning for her. You tell her I'm going to wring her neck."

She laughed. I heard her all the way till the house got out of sight and there wasn't anything left to hear except her laughter and my own shoe leather.

It took me three hours to get home. I went by one old church four times before I realized I didn't even know the way.

Another building I went by was this outfit called the 24-Hour Shopper's Bazaar. It was lit up like Jaycee's Fair. "Everything For the Home," the flashing lights said. I went in and bought a cake of soap, a box of breakfast cereal, and a full-size stuffed moose done in blue mohair.

The three girls were all asleep together in the one bed, their arms around one another. I turned off the lights which were blazing, and sat on the foot of the bed watching them. I sat staring, and thinking about them, how pretty they looked and how nice they could be when asleep. How they were always so nice when like this. They didn't look so unfaithful to me or as though they ever could be. And I was still there doing it when the sun came up.

Agnes sat up, rubbing her eyes. Her face was swollen with sleep and her hair all matted. She had this dirt circle all around her face. The room really did stink a little.

"Daddy?" she said. "Is that you, daddy?"

I kept on sitting there, nodding, smiling at her. I couldn't help it; I just liked hearing her call me "daddy" that much, like she was giving it back.

"Did you see mama?" she said. "Didn't she look terrific?"

I reached over and gave her a little love pat on the cheek. I tucked Monkey back in, who was about to roll out. She had a fistful of pebbles clenched in her little hand and I pried those loose. I fixed the covers up over Sarah's naked yellow foot. The sole was so black it looked like she'd been walking through tar. But it was a pretty little foot.

"Didn't she?" Agnes said. "Didn't she look fantastic?"

"She sure did," I said. "She's more beautiful now than she ever was. She's a wonderful woman, your mama is, and I'll never take that from her."

She got this quick black look over her face.

"Was she sleeping on a pallet in the kitchen?" she asked. She was practically yelling.

"Yessir," I said. "She was really sawing those logs."

Her look got blacker.

"Did she ask about us?" she said.

"She sure did," I said. "She sent you kids kisses and kisses."

This little remark nearly killed her. She sat gripping the covers and shaking. Her look was all blackness now. She could have got out of bed and walked on her lips. She was really stewing.

"She says you three kids are the greatest kids ever came

down the pike," I said. "She says she's going to stay faithful to
you kids come hell or high water."

Her fist shot out and slammed against my shoulder. Then
her legs started kicking. She kicked me about thirty hard
ones in the stomach and on my legs and all over, and all in
about one second.

"You fucking *daddy*!" she cried. "You big idiot! You liar!"

She leaped from the bed and went running into the bath.
She slammed the door and started screeching. I heard her
banging things around in there. First one item crashed and
then another.

I'd never seen her so hot-blooded.

After a while I put my eye to the keyhole. She had her own
eye there, looking back.

"I guess now you're going to be spending all your time over
at that Tucker woman's house," she said. "I guess you and our
mama are going to be billing and cooing."

"Not me," I said. "I'm going to be spending my time right
here with you three kids."

She seemed to brighten a bit. I grinned a shy little
grin at her.

"Come out now," I said. "Let's talk turkey."

She backed up. I saw her sit down on the edge of the tub and
cross her legs. She stayed there shivering and biting her lips.

"I hate this bathroom," she said. "We ought to take a
jackhammer to it."

"Okay by me," I said. "First thing tomorrow."

She began snatching out talk under her breath. I figured she
was cussing. Her face was all knotted up in rage.

"Mama has got fat," she said. "She's got fat and ugly."

"No, she hasn't," I said.

She cocked her head, listening. Then she jumped forward
and yanked the door open.

"You look like a fool," she said, "stooped at the keyhole
like that. I bet that's why mama left you." She dropped back

and sat down again on the tub ledge. "Why did she leave you?" she said.

"I don't know," I said. "Maybe she just found it too noisy around here. She couldn't find any peace of mind."

"I wouldn't put it past her," she said. "That would be just like her." She punched at my kneecap. "Why are you defending her?"

"I don't know," I said. "Maybe because she's not here to speak for herself."

She smiled in a quick bright way.

"That's right," she said. "She's over at that Tucker woman's house."

"Damn right!" I said. "Sawing those logs!"

She remained quiet a second, doping things out. Figuring out this and that.

"I heard she was packing," she said. "I heard she'd changed her mind about staying around here and was going to pack tonight and catch a train to Toledo."

"That's right," I said. "She mentioned that. She told me she was going to catch the first train to Toledo and enroll in law school."

Her eyebrows went up.

"Law school! Jesus Christ, daddy!"

"That's what she said. She aims to sit on the supreme-court bench before she's fifty."

Her skepticism gave way and she broke into a big grin.

"Good!" she said, standing up. "Get her out of the way. Get her where she can do no harm."

She marched back into the bedroom and scooted under the covers beside Sarah and Little Monkey. She was looking pretty alert now. She pointed toward the corner. "You've been to the 24-Hour Shopper's Bazaar," she said. "You'll have to take it back. That moose is too big and too ugly."

"You're absolutely right," I said. "I can see that moose just does not fit in."

"You can exchange it for a kitchen table," she said. "We kids don't like this house being so empty. We want some furniture."

"All right," I said. "Draw up a list."

She got this black look again.

"Me and the others here have been talking," she said. "We don't figure we've been exactly faithful to you. We don't figure we've been exactly faithful one little bit."

I felt this wet stuff sliding down my cheeks. I felt I never wanted to wipe it off.

"That's what we figure," she said.

"Yes you have," I said.

"You are a big liar," she said. "We have been crooked as the miles. We figure we're going to have to try a lot harder."

"I can too," I said. "We can all try harder. We can have real Family Nights around here. We can have a Parcheesie Night, a Scrabble Night, a Monopoly Night, maybe even a Strip-Poker Night."

"You don't know how" she said.

"Little Monkey can teach me," I said. "She can sit on my lap and teach me." I pulled up the cereal box I'd bought at the 24-Hour Shopper's Bazaar. "I bought you kids this new cereal," I said. "It says here on the box that kids of all ages love this dynamite new cereal."

She looked past it straight into my eyes.

"I'm never going to get married," she said. "If I do I hope someone will shoot me."

"We can have Ice-Cream and Chocolate-Cake Nights too," I said. "Every night."

"No, we can't," she said. "You're fixing to ruin us. You're fixing to turn us into fat, nasty, spoiled little brats."

"All right," I said. "When your sisters wake we will have us a family conversation. We will work out all of life's little problems."

"Fine," she said. "But Little Monkey gets a vote. Her vote counts the same as ours."

"Bet your life," I said. "Anybody tries taking away Little Monkey's vote they're going to be in a pack of trouble."

She smiled and opened her arms. I crawled on up and rooted out a place beside her. I was dead tired. That moose had weighed two hundred pounds. Sarah raised one sleepy eye and flopped an arm across my neck. Little Monkey was snoring.

"We're going to have to get her nose fixed," Agnes said. "It's crooked. That's why she snores like that."

"I'll call the bone surgeon right now," I said.

She patted my face. "Be still," she said. "Try to relax." I said okay. "I'm worried about mama," she said. "How can a person of her shortcomings ever make it through law school?"

"She'll make it," I said. "She'll be chairman of the board."

Agnes nestled up against me.

"Let's sleep now," she said. "Let's sleep our beauty sleep. Lord knows we need it. Let's let our minds go dead and think about absolutely nothing. Not about this house or mama in law school or Little Monkey's nose — not about anybody in the whole wide world. Let's stay here the whole day, sleeping and sleeping. Heck, we don't need to get up for a long time. Maybe we can stay here until next week."

"Amen," I said. "Oh brother, amen."

Sisters, too.

"Quiet!" said Agnes. "Keep quiet. Blot out everything except serene happiness. Are you doing it?"

"Yep. I'm doing it."

"Good. Move over, then. You're taking up too much bed. Quit crowding. Shift your arm. Pull up the covers. Don't let in drafts. Go to sleep now."

"I am," I said. "I'm sleeping now."

So the four of us stayed on sleeping, getting the hang on happiness.

It seemed we'd reached some kind of turning point in our lives.

It seemed we'd got there.

Saloam Frigid With Time's Legacy While Mrs. Willoughby Bight-Davies Sits Naked Through The Night On A Tree Stump Awaiting The Lizard That Will Make Her Loins Go Boom-Boom

THE MOMENT the crowded bus pulled out of the depot the woman seated beside Saloam placed a firm hand on his knee and said, "Do you have five dollars?" Saloam saw the face of a stout woman aged between fifty and sixty years, with no hair on her lips but with skin so sallow and roughened and eyes so green and jittery he thought immediately of a rocky hillside and of two large horseflies alight upon a cowpat. He had no interest whatsoever in talking to this person, or to anyone for that matter, inasmuch as today he was feeling notably antisocial and proud of it. Moreover, in all probability — and by way of explaining his current mood — he was, or soon expected to be, homeless, up a creek, cast out to the dogs.

All his ladylove's doings, which is what made it hurt so much.

His distaste for the woman beside him exceeded mere aversion; he felt something close to mortal offense at her insulting question.

"Sure, I got five dollars," he said. "What's it to you?"

The woman's smile broadened and only now — and now only after long interval — did she remove her hand from his knee.

"My name is Mrs. Willoughby Bight-Davies," she said. "Let me see this five dollars you say you have."

"Mind your own business," Saloam told her with all the patience he could muster. "I need my rest."

The woman slapped her knees, laughing at him. "I've heard it said when you're dead you can rest," she told him. "Right now you're sitting beside me."

Saloam let this pass. He looked out of the widow at the dismal rain and the shut-up city through which the bus was moving. He had been here three months working, since his ladylove last had chased him off. He was leaving behind nothing that he hoped ever to see again, and heading toward a future that might or might not exist. He wished he'd eaten breakfast and maybe bought a newspaper. He regretted he hadn't taken the time to make a few phone calls and tell a few people where they could get off. As for that future, where that was there was no phone. His ladylove did not believe in phones, and believed less in him. You're not for me, she often said. You can't cut it.

It broke his heart to admit it, but maybe she was right.

The green-eyed woman snapped her fingers in front of his face. "Are you dreaming?" she said. "Well I do like a dreamer. You do have five dollars, don't you? Let's see it."

It filled Saloam with remorse that he had to share seats with such a repellent person. She was too jolly and too talky and exactly the kind he found most loathsome in all the world.

"Five dollars!" she hooted. "Pennies from heaven! Out with it, young man!"

She snapped her fingers, her eyes not swaying once from his.

Crazy, Saloam thought. She's come down out of the tree. He reasoned that he was seated either beside some nut or beside some kind of weird magician-type person who meant to perform a trick with his five dollars. Maybe a flimflammer. But if she meant to try stealing money off him she was in for a big letdown. She would end up with a big foot in her face.

"Don't be poky," she said.

After much squirming and shifting about and not wanting to

do it, Saloam succeeded in extracting a five-dollar bill from the wallet in his hip pocket. He held it firmly between his fingers and floated it by her face.

"Now that's five dollars," he said. "I got lots more where that came from."

She watched it float.

"I'm sure you do," she said smiling. "Let me hold it."

For a few intense seconds they struggled over the note, the woman rippling with laughter, Saloam resisting a desire to crack his elbow into her ribs. She was a good deal stronger than he had imagined, and a good deal more determined. But he wasn't about to surrender his money.

"Let go!" he cried.

"You," she said. "That's Common-Market money, good for the rich and the poor!"

Saloam did not have time to consider what she meant by this. Her own elbow cracked into his ribs. The bill floated free and she plucked it out of the air. "Now that's magic for you," she laughed. "That's how magic works. That's how a woman gets hold of a stubborn five-dollar bill!" She said this in a voice not modified in the least by the presence of forty-six other passengers on the bus, many of whom were twisting their necks to see what the ruckus was about. Across the aisle two children of vaguely Oriental description were staring at him, open-mouthed but silent, making wild signals with their fingers. Saloam ignored them.

"Thank you," the woman said. "Now for that five dollars I shall tell you my life story."

Saloam snatched back his five dollars. He shot it up under his coat and stuffed it inside his shirt pocket.

"Lady," he said. "I never met *any* person whose life story was worth five dollars. I wouldn't give five dollars for the pope's life story, much less yours."

The woman nodded serenely at this, adjusting her voluminous clothing, making no effort to retrieve his currency.

"You're Catholic then," she said, patting his knee.

Saloam, seated with his long black overcoat twisted beneath him, lifted himself up and tugged the coat collar up around his head. His wool muffler was slung over his shoulder and he caught both ends and yanked it tight around his neck. He slid low into the seat and propped up his knees. He would have smoked but for forty-six others who were going at it like fire engines.

"No," he said, "I hope to God I'm not Catholic. I wouldn't give five cents for any Catholic on the face of this universe."

A heavy-set man to Saloam's front reared up over his seat back, examining Saloam with a menacing scowl. "Keep it to yourself, sonny boy," he said. "Watch it or you might get your lips busted."

Saloam looked down at his feet. He had the sudden fear that this journey was going to be a long and miserable one, in which anything might happen. He'd arrive worn out, too dead on his feet to stand up to his ladylove's venom.

The woman picked his hand up off his lap and stroked it. She spoke, to Saloam's mind, with a strange gentleness. "You don't need to show your brusque side to me, young man," she said. "Under that indifferent and rude facade I know inside you're nice as kittens."

This remark quite amazed Saloam, and secretly pleased him. In this rare instance the absurd pest beside him had shown a lot more perspicacity than most he could name, including his ladylove.

"You don't know what you're saying," he replied sullenly. "I don't ask nothing from nobody, and that goes for Catholics."

It hurt him to keep harping on this note since it verged on a betrayal: his ladylove was part Catholic.

"Never you mind," the woman said. She had her purse up from the floor and was scrutinizing her face in a tiny gold compact mirror.

"I was born in a small village you never heard of," she began, "in a country you never heard of either, since it does not now exist and in fact went the way of Moses and his tribe long before you were born. I was the fourth child, the second *girl* child, in a family numbering nine, three boys and four girls, plus my parents. My sisters' names were Clolde, Izelde, and Gezelde, and my brothers were named after a great sweep of uncles and great-uncles on my father's side. Do you want to know their names? My father, who was older than my mother by a good many years, not an arrangement to be encouraged, had come from one of the many neighboring villages and by local standards had got along very well. We were poor and toothless much of the time but respectable. We had ground which we could work and which provided us with some little bounty, in addition to fresh table vegetables. Later on, about the time of my birth, my father supplemented his income through employment at a nearby dairy. He worked long hard hours and was greatly loved by all concerned. My mother, whose health —''

Saloam bolted up and lurched angrily down the aisle to the lavatory at the rear. Jesus Christ and Mary, he said under his breath.

The door would not open.

"It's out of whack. Out of commission," someone said.

Saloam swore. In all his travels, whatever the bus line, night or day, he'd yet to find a bus toilet in working order. He stood fuming, hands clenched in his pockets.

"It's shut up," the same voice said. "That toilet's gone fishing."

Some of the idiots seated there laughed.

"Come back on Sunday," another wit said. "After the evening service."

Saloam, to have something to do, rattled the door.

"The confessional box will then be open."

Saloam groaned.

"What that man needs," came the first voice again, "is a bottle."

To Saloam's disgust this idiotic remark unleashed a wave of

chuckles. Saloam had certain ideas about a person's dignity; it was clear to him that this crew didn't. Stooping, he stared out of the windows at the slush and rain and black trees swishing by. Awful. It was awful out there, wet enough to drown a cat. He hoped it wasn't raining where he was going. His ladylove was tops, a good woman, the light of his life, but she might very well throw him right out in it. Right out, without giving him a chance. "Your promises," she'd say, "don't amount to nothing."

"What is it this time?" she'd say. "Potency pills?"

He dropped back miserably into his seat beside the talkative green-eyed woman.

She thrust a photograph into his hands the instant he landed. ". . . whose health, I was saying," she went on, "was on the frail side, had her hands full looking after so many children. That snapshot shows the entire family." She pointed. "Here is my father with his cap on and in his Sunday suit — isn't he touching? — and down at this far end, nursing the youngest — Gezelde, that would be — is my mother. Isn't it amazing how frail she looks? I am this one up here by the door with my mouth open. I was thirteen the year this was taken, and was already betrothed. That is his shadow you see behind me. His name was Frederico and he was the most darling boy imaginable. He called me his Little Dumpling and tried to make me do terrible things with him. He was dead set against marriage though, and was only led to the altar when he got another girl, a friend of mine, into trouble. Do you know what I mean? She was a dim-witted girl and not very pretty. We all laughed when it happened. My father said it showed the kind of man that Frederico was, that he was willing to marry her, this friend of mine, when she wasn't the least bit desirable. I died of a broken heart but it very quickly mended, because there were any number of very earnest boys after me. My mother said that such a thing could never happen in our family, because we were very strict, you see, and had right from wrong drummed into us from the very beginning. It turned out, however, that my oldest sister, Clolde — that was Clolde back there with the stick in her mouth and one foot up scratching her leg — was already in the family way. The object of her passion was an extremely dense but good-looking boy who was all the rage in our village. When Clolde could hide her condition no longer she cried and cried. We all cried, even my father, because it was very sad and because we all had high hopes for Clolde who everyone agreed was the family beauty. One morning we waked to find her bed had not been slept in and we went on a great hunt for her person. The boy said he had not seen her. He denied any knowledge of her whereabouts and swore that he had never never touched her. He was in love, you see, with the apothecary's daughter, who was no beauty but had a bit of wealth behind her. We did not hear from Clolde until a full year had gone by, whereupon it was disclosed that she had taken a job as a domestic in the city and had there married an elderly and kind-hearted fisherman. The reason this is important is that Clolde advised my parents that I should also come to the city because there was great opportunity there for one of my talents, together with numerous boys who seemed not to know what to do with themselves. When my parents told me of this I —''

Saloam hove up dramatically from his seat and strode as fast as he could to the front of the bus. The green-eyed woman had a peculiarly infuriating voice, brazen and not the least melodi-ous and — worse yet — she was constantly grabbing at him, or elbowing him, or shaking a ridiculous finger into his face. His groans, his grimaces, his indifference and breathy swearings, had no effect whatsoever on her. *That's* a life story! he thought. That dishwater! Christ, she ought to hear mine!

He stood watching the highway unfold through the large windshield, watched the droning wipers and the slush pitched up by the cars and the big trailer trucks in front, and though this bored him mercilessly he did not know what else to do. In addition to which, even bundled up in muffler and long coat, with thick woolen underwear over the length of his body, he was shivering with cold, with cold and a thousand frustrations. He was indignant that he had to listen to that woman — enraged by the whole affair, including how his ladylove done him. He loathed every passenger on the bus for their dull and docile, remorseless behavior; he wished he could wring the necks of each of these contented barbarians, starting with Green-eyes. They deserved the empty, stupid lives that awaited them at the end of the line. But did he? Hadn't he tried his best? Didn't his ladylove know that? Oh, yes. Yes yes yes, that was three-quarters of his predicament. She knew it. He adored her, had put her on a pedestal. He was her slave and she knew it. But why not? His ladylove was angelic, wonderful, so fiery — such a sexy creature! His hands shook at the mere thought that within a few hours these hands might possibly be touching her. Possibly. Such skin! Such radiance! Would she let him? Or would she fling his hands aside? "Do you dare touch me!" Would she say that? "Do you dare touch me, you vassal, you niggler, when your seed can only float on water? When my womb is a tomb that can only stay empty? What good are you to me? I want babies! If it was sponge cake I wanted I'd go to my kitchen. Get out! Go! Disappear!"

He became aware, by degrees, of the driver's stern gaze on him in the rearview mirror.

"You can't stand there," the driver said manfully. "Get back to your seat."

Saloam lunged forward and scooped down on his heels beside the man's chair. Bud, the driver's name was. It said so behind yellow plastic up over the windshield. "There's a crazy woman back there," Saloam said, jerking a thumb. "She won't shut up."

Through the rearview glass the driver probed at length the mysterious depth of his bus.

"Looks normal to me," he said. "Looks harmless. Return to your seat. Now!"

"She's stark raving mad!" argued Saloam. "She tried stealing my money!"

The driver stretched one arm across his wheel and drove the other stiffly against Saloam's shoulder. "Take it easy, buster," he said. "You look like the crazy one to me."

Saloam went rigid. There was no fairness in this world, not anywhere.

"Get back or get off. Don't talk to me. You see that sign? That sign says 'No Talking To Driver While Bus Is In Motion.' It says 'Smoking Prohibited' and no carrying of firearms or explosives and a lot of other things, but mostly it says you get your ass back to your seat. You read me? Am I coming in loud and clear?"

Saloam, defeated, stared at a pint-sized image of the Virgin Mary adorning the bus panel, protected by the dusty chrome fence which encircled her. Inside the fence, against her base, was a pile of nickels and dimes. The pope's money.

Saloam snarled and whirled away.

He paused beside a number of riders, inquiring whether they would object to exchanging seats — pointing back to specify the empty chair beside the smiling lady with the green eyes, who that moment was biting into an apple and nodding violently — but those Saloam accosted either said nothing or turned away or spoke in a grumbling language which he could not understand.

Afghan, maybe. Maybe Sudanese. The whole bus load looked like a gang of misfits headed for a convict colony.

The two boys looked expectantly at him, their sallow faces beaming. They had slick black hair and ears that were pressed flat; they looked more than vaguely Oriental. Their yellow hands tumbled and turned.

Saloam fell resentfully into his seat.

The woman had a white paper napkin spread over her lap, bordered in green holly, like Christmas. She placed the apple core at its center, neatly folded the four corners, and tucked the result away inside her fat purse.

"Bus drivers are the most terrifying individuals alive," she said. "They strike terror into the human heart. This, I believe, is because they lead such sordid, eventful lives."

"Oh shut up," Saloam said.

"Now you," she said. "I can tell you have troubles in your life. You have a bankrupt, unhopeful demeanor. I can tell there's a woman in your life. What's her name?"

"Ladylove," Saloam quietly muttered.

The woman sagely nodded. "This is a new age, however," she said. "The dawn of a new age. We must never surrender to our bitter nature. We must make do, and if that doesn't work, God forbid, we must make ourselves over."

Saloam shifted furiously in his seat. Now a lecture. He wrenched and thrashed and crossed his knees, thumping the seat in front. The man there who had defended the Catholics rose up a second time, glaring solemnly.

"You ought to study the lives of the saints," he said. 'The lives of the saints would open your eyes to a fact or two."

Saloam twisted away, flinging his legs out into the aisle. The children's hands were fluttering wildly, their eyes joyful and lidded; except for their tumbling hands they were absolutely motionless. Comprehension came to Saloam. There were deaf and dumb children. They were deaf and dumb, poor little rats, and only doing what deaf and dumb children had to do, which was to talk a mile a minute with their hands and try not to look like it was killing them.

The woman pawed his arm.

"So I went to the city," she said, "and lived with my sister and her husband, the fisherman, and although most of the people I met were as good to me as if I were their very own daughter this did not work out and you may well ask me why. It was because I was so homesick I cried myself to sleep each night. I was greatly missing my darling Frederico who found he did not get along at all well with his rich wife and in recompense had been petitioning me on the sly to do a great many very dirty things with him. I wouldn't, though he was a peck of fun, a joy was Frederico who could constantly make me laugh. I teased him no end but would never allow him to touch me except by what we termed an accident, and in addition there were numerous other earnest boys who took delight in my company. But in the city there was absolutely no one my age who paid me the slightest attention and I did not strongly favor my sister's husband who was of a despondent and melancholy nature and ever grumbling that if he had but money for a boat he could stop working for others and grow rich and retire and never have to lift finger again. My sister was no comfort either because she seemed to me to be a thousand years old, with children always hanging from her and her breasts always in someone's mouth and always at me to sweep the floor or otherwise make myself useful. So I fled home to my village, encouraged to do so because my father was ill and my poor mother could not manage. Frederico continued to harass me and one evening at my parents' house he produced a bottle of potato wine which he had made himself and although it was bitter and not to my liking I drank it and sat on his lap and to my considerable vexation allowed him to kiss me. He breathed into and tickled my ear and succeeded in getting his hand under my vest, whereupon he caressed me endlessly. I was of two minds about this, but it was as if I had three hearts, one inside me and beating, and two others upon my chest which took the beat when his hands went to them, and this I found most exhilarating. I chided him that he was a married man, I upbraided him, but I confess I also kissed him wantonly. Nay, I kissed him with reckless abandon. I kissed his ears and mouth and neck and for some little minutes allowed him to do with me as he wished. You will understand that this was the high and low points of my life up to that hour, and my yearnings, not to mention my satisfaction, caused me massive conflict of conscience for many years to come. You will of course have been in such situations yourself, from the male side of the spectrum, and you will know precisely what I mean."

Saloam shuddered, regarding her with cold fury.

"I never," he said. "I never had no dealings with married women. I strictly avoid married women, and as far as that goes, women in general. I live only for my one ladylove's pleasure."

He could have cut out his tongue. He knew what mincemeat his ladylove would make of this declaration. She would say his pitching and wallowing over her, his endless cooing, was as sick and unholy as it was all to no avail. "Your seed is without honor," she'd say. "Get up, get out."

The woman clutched his knee. "When I say I let Frederico do what he wished," she gushed, smiling coyly, "I do not mean to suggest that I let him go hog-wild, or do anything unforgivable. No, Frederico was not that kind of person, though he certainly liked his potato wine and was most assuredly given to fondling, nipping, and kissing. He had my clothes ripped off me and got more than an eyeful, but he was hardly the sort of wanton savage that would take unkind advantage. No. Though I put it to you simply: I was fully prepared to throw caution to the winds, and take my medicine."

Once again Saloam heaved himself up and strode the aisle. This wretched creature's story was endless. It was endless and pointless and next to obscene.

"Phooey!" he said.

He hugged his coat and muffler to his body and glared at the deaf and dumb children whose fingers were interminably spinning. Telling their own life stories, he supposed. Telling it to the weak, uncaring air.

He stared with hatred at the lavatory's locked door. No refuge, no relief, no exit.

The people seated along the aisle did not even concede him this space; they left their feet spread for him to trip over. They regarded his passage through somber, heavy lids, clearly displeased by his existence. Cold air poured around him.

"Five more hours," one of these cretins said, to no one in particular.

"*You!*" came the driver's voice in a rustle of static. "Take your seat!"

Saloam obeyed. Why not? His life was crushed anyhow. His ladylove was just too tough on him. She excused nothing.

The woman at once took up her story. The four hands of the deaf and dumb children hooked into high gear.

Saloam felt sick with depression.

"Years went by," she said, "and any number of very earnest boys were ever chasing me. I took up with a nice lad I met on the bridge and we were married in due time under a shed on the place where his family lived high in the mountains. A fine Sunday this was, with relatives in to play the accordian. Oh, the songs I heard that day! I was so happy. We killed and consumed numerous chickens. I tell you I will never forget that day if I live to be a thousand years. Phillippe was that boy's name, and very sweet he was too, giving in to my every whim. Doting on me. He was a powerfully built little lad who worked from sunup to sunset in the fields, and daily I would trudge up the mountain to deliver him his hot lunch, for I doted on him as well and much admired his physique and could not get enough of his kisses. I was immensely proud of myself and much enamored of my new station in life. I would bear him a thousand children, I thought, and they would all be called Phillippe."

Saloam drew the muffler tight against his ears. He slid horizontally into the seat, twisting his legs, yanking the coat up over his head. He kept his eyes open, however, and through a narrow slit of daylight saw that the man to his front had again risen to address him.

"No more of that anti-Catholic talk," the man said. "The

lives of the saints! You study the lives of the saints, my boy, then you'll sing a different tune. The lives of the saints will give you something to shoot for.''

Saloam, fists knotted, said nothing.

The man was not yet finished. "It's never too late!" he said. "Millions come to the faith even at age eighty. In the end that's what it comes to: the faith can save you. The saints! Study the saints!''

Floating through Saloam's mind in a general way was some vague idea about eternal injustice and how it never varied; about how he wouldn't mind if this bus veered suddenly off the road and tumbled over a cliff, leaving no one except himself to walk away. Including whatever saints might be riding. He was dwelling on this and on his ladylove and what she might say upon his arrival. "An apparition!" she'd say. "Why have you come back, meaningless apparition? Get up, get out, stay away! What makes you think it will be different this time? Your seed is weary, your seed is ignoble. You have no seed. Abandon my threshold!''

"But I could not have children," the woman said touching his arm. "Year after besieged year my stomach stayed flat, and because of this wicked condition my dear Phillippe renounced his vows and abandoned me. He took up with my middle sister Iselde, who was a sweet person but not all there, to make no bones about it. She was a good deal like Phillippe, I mean to say — both of them very sweet and adoring above all else the generous nest of family. I didn't blame either of them, for how could I? — but how I cried and cried that I could not bear in my loins a darling child. 'Barren, oh barren!' I cried, moaning through my village under this curse. I went to see a woman who lived far down the road, in a vile cave she was said to live, in a neck of woods into which the people of my village rarely ventured. They practiced deadly voodoo, you see, down this road, and many brave souls who did so venture often were never to be seen again. Have not to this day. But I went, for I

was derogate and without hope, a stain on my pathway to
oblivion. But wait! I was told that down this road lived a certain
aged and infirm woman, part witch, who was known to have
cures for all ailments, including what a humbled girl should do
who was unable to conceive and bear children. Yes, you may
well look at me with kindled interest, for it is the honest truth
as I am here to tell you.''

Saloam's head had crept up. His brows were together, his
mouth open, his eyes strangely hooded.

The children across the aisle tumbled their fingers with
excessive vigor, their faces alert with cunning excitement.

"What a hovel she lived in!" continued the woman. "I tell
you I was frightened out of my wits and sorely beside myself
with dread and apprehension. But I was so desperate I did
exactly as that haggard creature said. First, I should give her
my coins. Then I should kiss her feet. Then I should go into the
forest and find a mossy stump, and I should sit naked through
the night upon this stump without one thought of fleeing.''

Saloam looked hard at the woman. It seemed to him that her
green eyes had deepened. Her eyes seemed to him to be two
swirling holes cut out of the rain-splattered window.

Deaf and dumb hands spun as though in ecstacy.

"At sunrise, she told me, a baby lizard would run from
beneath this stump and I must catch this lizard with one quick
hand and while on my knees plop it living and squiggling into
my mouth and I must swallow it whole and race without
stopping to my lodgings away in my village and there I should
drink three full dippers of pure well water over which I had
first intoned as a matter of necessity several special and
significant words.''

The woman's recitation stopped. She lifted her purse and
took from it an unsoiled paper tissue and noisily blew her nose.

Saloam squirmed.

"What is it?" she asked him. "Am I to understand I now
have your attention?''

Saloam wiped both hands over his face. He rubbed his eyes and stared giddily at her.

"What special words?" he said.

The woman cocked her head at the two children across the aisle. They were up on their knees in the seats, heads side by side, grinning, their hands at soft rest against the cushions.

"What words?" urged Saloam. "For God's sake, get on with your story."

The man in front of Saloam reared up. "Oh, it's for God's sake now, is it?" he said.

The woman sat relaxed, hands in her lap, her knees together. She was oddly smiling. She gazed idly out of the window and up at the overhead racks, and daydreamily picked fluff from her voluminous skirts. She drummed her fingers against the aluminum window framing and toyed with the light. She shifted her feet and scratched one knee. She hummed. Time is so tedious and life so slow, she seemed to be saying. What an endless, boring journey this is that I am on, she seemed to be saying.

Miserably, Saloam rooted out the five-dollar note from his pocket. He placed it down on her lap.

"I had you figured out a long time ago," he said. "Once you got hold of my five dollars you'd shut up. Otherwise, you'd talk my ears off. You probably make a trillion dollars pulling this trick and I wouldn't be surprised to find that's why you are on this bus. But okay. You're not outsmarting me. There's your five dollars. It happens I want to hear your story. Some of it. Go back to that lizard part. That stump. Go back to that part about the barren womb. Don't leave out any details, including those special and significant words. *Especially* including those."

The woman folded up the five-dollar bill.

"You're a nasty talker out of nasty habit," she said, not unkindly. "Nasty talking induces nasty thinking as much as it does the other way around, and I would suggest you work on that. Your ladylove can't like it."

She folded the bill, with firm creases, twelve times by Saloam's count. She placed it in her palm and closed her fist upon it. Saloam saw the bill emerge a second later up between two fingers; it flowed snakelike between her fingers, over and under. Then it was again hidden inside her closed fist.

The two boys were down in the aisle, pressing against Saloam, delightedly watching.

She smiled up at them. She opened both hands and lay the fingers flat; the bill had disappeared.

One of the boys shook Saloam's shoulder. He looked into Saloam's eyes, touched a hand behind his own ear; he then extended his arm. The five-dollar bill floated under Saloam's nose.

Saloam groaned. For all he knew, the entire bus was filled with magicians. If not magicians, then Catholics. Perhaps they were a delegation from the church, on their way to verify this or that miracle. He squinted unhappily at the smiling woman, thinking about her life story. He could hear the tires humming over the highway and muck swishing up against the under-pinning. Rain and dirt and slush smeared the windows.

The toilet flushed in the rear.

The driver honked his horn, gearing up to pass.

"You got my dough," Saloam growled. "Let's hear it."

The woman sat undisturbed, as if off in slumbrous heaven. She spoke without turning. She had a new note in her voice, soft and deep and a little reluctant.

"The price of my total life story, for certain anti-religious gentlemen," she said, "is now considerable more than five inconsequential dollars."

The man to Saloam's front hoisted his head around.

"You tell him, lady. You clue him in on the saints."

Saloam held firm. "How much more?" he said. "For all that stuff about the lizards and the special words and such?"

"Twenty dollars total," she said. "Twenty might get us to our destination."

Saloam flushed out his wallet and peeled off the bills.

"Okay," he said. "I'm listening. Get to it." He stretched his legs, lowered himself into the seat, and closed his eyes.

"I visited this fearsome person, as I told you," said the woman. "This witch. She bade me enter a forest and sit naked upon a stump through the long night. I was to snare a young lizard that would be beneath this stump."

"I know that part," broke in Saloam. But he sounded content.

"She bade me swallow the lizard without compromise and rush forthwith to my abode. I was to draw three full dippers of pure fresh well water and intone over it several special and magical words. I was to drink this water and ere the next full moon arose I would be with child. I did all this."

"What were these magical words?" Saloam asked softly.

"Ere the next moon arose I indeed was with child. In time to come I bore the twin angels you see there. My village anointed me and titled me 'Mother Of All Wombs' and gave me the name 'Willoughby Bight-Davies,' for this was the name of a good and noble gentleman whose landholdings extended from river to river and mountain to mountain, over a range embracing ten thousand hectares."

"The words," begged Saloam. "What were the words?"

"*Saloam est saloam,*" breathed the woman. "*Saloam est saloam est saloam, est lema saloam Eloi, Eloi, sabachthani!*"

Saloam groaned pleasurably. He groaned under the full weight of his name, feeling that no longer was he ridiculous.

"*Saloam est saloam?*" he said.

The woman nodded.

Across the aisle the boys' hands were flying. They spun and leaped and flipped, and at last fell silent. Contentment came to Saloam as he fixed the woman's words into his memory. It might work. Why not? It fit. He'd tell Ladylove. They'd try it.

"Now that was chapter one," the woman said. "You want to hear another? Are you willing to pay for it?"

Saloam placed his wallet in the woman's lap. He placed it there without pause, looking at her tenderly — looking at her, indeed, as if he loved her.

The woman's story went on.

Her story amazed Saloam. He was amazed with himself as well. He was struck with joy by what he beheld as his future.

Saks Fifth Avenue

A WOMAN CALLED ME up on the telephone. She was going to give me twenty thousand dollars, she said. I said come right over, I'm not doing anything this evening. Then I went back into the living room where my wife was, seated on the sofa with her nail files and paint, painting her nails. I wanted to keep it to myself for a bit. I strolled around, pawing the knickknacks, glancing now and then at myself in the mirror. I was feeling pretty breezy.

Twenty thousand, I thought. Holy Christ!

Those knickknacks were really dusty; I had to go in and wash my hands. While I was in there, in the bathroom, I splashed on a little cologne and smiled at myself. There are going to be some changes around here, is what I told myself. These old mirror tiles got to go.

The old lady looked up. She'd finished her left hand, which she always does first, God knows why. Her nails were the vilest colour I ever saw — dried blood. What they call Songbird Red in the ads. Songbird Red: how about that? It's her favorite color for nails. Also, she says it protects them, and keeps her from chewing.

So she looked up. "You're smirking," she said. "God, I hate it when you smirk. Why don't you go get us a beer?"

I went into the kitchen and got the beer.

"Thanks," she said. "You look like you swallowed a monkey.

It's disgusting. You disgust me, Cecil.'' She folded her fingers over and blew on the songbirds. Then she fluttered her fingers. I watched her do it. That's a pretty sexy act, that nail-blowing act. It's about as sexy as anything I can imagine. Seeing old Coolie blow on her nails is enough to make me forgive her for all of her sins, including how she talks to me.

Coolie, I forgive you.

Coolie, you set my heart a-racing.

Coolie, let's go to bed.

Silly, but that's how it is. I was really feeling mellowed out.

"Well?" she said. "Why the honey-licking grin? Why don't you take a walk? Polish your shoes, do something! You're full of yourself this evening. God knows why, after the way you behaved last night.''

She said a lot of stuff like that. Once she gets going you never know when she's going to wind down. I figure she doesn't even hear herself. She talks to her mother — to her mother and her girl friends — that same way. They never slow down. They don't even hear each other.

"Stop pacing, Cecil,'' she said.

I got out my shoes and the polish box. We keep the polish — the white and the neutral, blacks and reds and tans, and a tin of Arctic Dubbin that must have been in there fifteen years — in a thick white cardboard box that says "Saks Fifth Avenue.'' I always look at that box. I try to figure out what must have come in that box. How we came to have it. It's one of the mysteries of my life, that box. I look at it and sometimes wonder if old Coolie hasn't had a life I don't know about.

That's deep, deep business, but I get that way sometimes. I can be watching TV for instance, the old prime time, and right out of the blue that thought will come to me: how'd we get that box? Where did it come from? What was in it? Sometimes I'll look up and find the show ending, and I've been thinking about that box the whole hour.

"Can you believe it!'' Coolie will say. "Why do they

show trash like that? Wasn't that the most impossible crap you ever saw?"

"I don't know, Coolie," I say. "That car chase was pretty good."

She gives me this level gaze. "You are totally without taste," she says. "They make this crap for imbeciles like you."

I mention this box business as an example of the kind of secret life that some of us have. How you can pass old Joe Blow on the street, have a conversation with him, even a real interesting one, and then you walk away wondering what the heck either of you said.

I mean we don't even hear each other.

So I got out the box. I couldn't decide which pair needed doing, the loafers or the old cowboy boots. None of them really needed it. What the loafers needed was new heels.

"These heels are worn down," I told Coolie. "Look at these heels."

She didn't look.

"How long have I had these shoes?" I asked her. "I bet I had these shoes a good ten years. Did I ever ask you where this Saks box came from? That one's going to drive me crazy if I don't figure it out."

"Would you shut up?" said Coolie. "Would you please hush your mouth?"

She'd gone back to painting her other fingers. She had her tongue between her lips and sat all bunched over, scrunched up tight, with her right hand spread out over her knees and this look of utter concentration on her face. I'd noticed that tongue before. Usually she's biting down on it with her teeth, the upper lip curled back, but tonight she just had it hanging there. Squinting, because she had her contacts out. She was wearing this pink gown I got for her one Christmas eve at K-Mart, and she had it flung back away from her knees so no paint would get on it. None of that Songbird Red.

It had already got pretty grimy, that gown. I don't think

she's washed it once. I find this odd, and maybe a little bit out of character, her always wearing that filthy gown, because she's got this idea she's the sharpest dresser in town. "And on my budget!" — is what she's always saying.

"Would you stop looking at me!" she says now. "Would you stop it! Would you put a lid on it!"

What I figure is it's just like Coolie is. It's how she talks. Say when she's with her girl friends or with her mother, she doesn't hear herself or them. They don't either. I've never understood a word, not a word, any of them have said. You come into the room and they are all eating cake and clattering cups and all going at once. Not even a pause for breath. It beats me. I'm really fascinated by it.

"What did they say?" I'll ask her once everyone has gone. "What were you talking about?"

She'll give me her withering look. "Oh you're such a dope," she'll say. "Oh, Cecil, you are the world's prize dope. Don't concern yourself. Go on with your life. Go out and rake the yard."

Maybe I am a dope. Maybe they do hear each other. But I got my doubts. I'm going to hold onto my doubts. I figure it's like that gown. She doesn't *know* how grimy that gown is. To her, all that dirt is invisible. She'd be mortally offended if I took a notion to drop hints. *"Are you calling me dirty, Cecil! Are you saying I am unclean!"* No, she grabs that gown off the hook every evening, she whips it on and comes running downstairs, and that's the end of it.

"Damnit, Cecil!" she says now. "Stop staring! Haven't I told you? I'm going to throw this bottle at you!"

That bottle. That little bottle of nail polish. What I really wanted was for that bottle to spill over, dribble over her knees and down her leg and spot the carpet. Spot it real nice. Then when people ask me what colour that carpet is I could say, well, some of it is Songbird Red. Some of it is.

Coolie would kill me, but I'd say it anyhow.

A little drama, you see, is what I wanted. A bit of cold, hard action. For if old Coolie accidentally knocked over that polish she'd leap up screeching, turning over tables and slamming the knickknacks about, and go on flapping her arms for a full ten minutes.

That's how Coolie is. Pretty high-strung. I love it when old Coolie goes into her screeching routine.

Those little bottles are insane. That's what I think. Big white cap built like a finger, with a nail two inches long. Painted Songbird Red. Dried blood. Quite a knickknack itself, that bottle. I sat there watching her dab the color on her nails, wondering how many of those little bottles it would take to paint the house. How *long* it would take, using that stupid brush. What the house would look like done up in a dynamite dried blood. Songbird Red.

About fifty million, I thought.

Take about twenty-seven years.

Coolie flipped the gown up over her knees. Groaned. She figured I had been staring at her naked knees. Getting an eyeful of the famous Coolie legs. Getting ideas.

"Last night," she said. "Last night. We just won't speak of last night."

She gave me this long look. Long, *mean*, and intense. "No," that look said. "Last night is not to be spoken of. We'd best, both of us, forget last night."

She was right, too. Last night we'd had a bit of erotica around here. A dab of it. Pretty high-powered stuff, too, for a while. Kissing and fondling — hell, *rapture*, if you want to know the truth.

"Kiss me, Cecil! Kiss me till my mouth bursts into flames!"

A *hot* time, I'm saying, and straight out of right field. She came in at five, said, "Cecil, mix us a drink." At ten after, she said, "Lead the way." A minute later there's that "mouth-into-flames" line. And no doubt about it, either. Sparks all over the place. Erotic *art*, for God's sake. Then the phone rings. Coolie snatches it up. "Not now!" she says. She starts to slam it back down and is already rolling into me, but the voice is chattering on. "What?" says Coolie. "What?" And she's got that phone back at her ear. "Six glasses for fourteen ninety-five? Long-stemmed! Gold-rimmed! That's unheard of! You're sure?"

But not only glassware, it seems.

"Fur coats at half price! *Shoes!* Did you say *shoes!*"

I roll away. Reach for something to read. There's *Redbook*. Well, by God, I'll read *Redbook* — that's what I say to myself. It's a jam-packed issue, too. I could spend a month just turning the pages.

"Blues and greens!" Coolie says. "They've got them in blues and greens! At twelve-eighty-*eight*! Jesus, mother!"

So I get up. I have a long shower. I go downstairs and make myself a roast beef. I have four or five hard drinks. I sponge the counter. Get the garbage taken out. Read the paper.

"I've got to go, mother," I hear Coolie saying. "Cecil's sulking."

Half an hour later they are still going strong. Not even hearing each other.

Well, it's getting dark. It's way *past* dark. Heck, in another minute or two it will be morning. But they are still going at it.

So I get dressed. I get on the old cowboy boots and go for a walk. All over the neighborhood. Maybe ten or twelve miles. When I get back old Coolie is standing in the open doorway. She's got on her grimy robe. She's patting her foot.

"You son of a bitch!" she says. And she whirls and strides away.

No. We best not speak of last night. We best let that sleeping dog stay where he is.

What I say is: thank God for the nail polish. That little act, for the moment, has taken care of both our emotional needs. I checked my watch. The woman on the phone had said she'd be over about eight. Give or take a few minutes. She'd be bringing the money with her. Every last dollar.

I was thinking I might mention this to Coolie. I was thinking she might want to run a comb through her hair. Maybe step into that hotshot pantsuit she got at Zellers. Got for practically nothing, I might add. What they did was they had this big flashing green light went off every hour, and if you were one of the first five thousand to rush over in the next five minutes then you could get this great pantsuit for practically nothing. The "Green-Light Special," they called it. Coolie got two of them, one black and the other a kind of orange. I hadn't seen her wearing that black one yet. I figured it either didn't fit — too tight in the hips is what it usually was — or she was saving it for something special. Tonight it might be just what the doctor ordered. She'd want to look snazzy for that woman coming over with the money.

I was going to say something along these lines, but Coolie beat me to the punch. She got in her two bits first.

"Supper tonight was terrible," she said. "You can't do casseroles. I wish you wouldn't even try. Your cooking has sure gone downhill. I've been sitting here thinking of what you cook and what I let go into my stomach, and the whole thing makes me sick. I can't bear to think of it. Christ, for once can't you follow a recipe?"

My face went a little hard at this. I'm touchy about my cooking. There was nothing wrong with my casserole.

Anyway, she ate it. Had seconds, too.

"I mean it," she said. "If I eat another casserole in this house I will puke. I will. I think I will die."

She started that nail-blowing act again. She'd put on a second coat.

Bless you, Coolie, I thought. You are such a wizard.

She straightened her two hands up in front of her face, flipped them over, flipped them back, then shot out her arms and bent her wrists and squinted long-range at those fingers. Then she shook them.

She kept on doing that.

I shaded my face and watched. It was better than TV. It had prime time beat by a mile. I was thinking of bones. Thinking of a woman's bones and how old Coolie could fold her hands down until they practically lay alongside her wrists. Fold them back the same. Supple as a shoe rag.

Well, they are contortionists, that's what they are.

Wizards, from head to toe.

"God, you make me sick," Coolie said. "I don't know what I am to do with you. My mother's right, you know. You know what she said? Only the other day she said to me, 'Coolie, what your husband needs is a pacemaker. A good pacemaker, secondhand.' Seriously, that's what she said. 'Otherwise,' she said, 'otherwise, someone is going to mistake him for dead. You're going to come home one day from work and find men in white coats rolling him out of there.' It's true, too, Cecil. You're going to be mistaken for the dead."

She said that, but she wasn't looking at me. First she was looking at the bottle, then at her feet, then at the nail polish again. She was trying to figure out whether she wanted to paint her toes. She couldn't decide. Should I or should I not? She has this little argument with herself about once a week. Sometimes the toenails win and sometimes they lose.

"What do you think?" she said. "Should I?"

If I say don't, then she will paint them. If I say do, she will look at me as if I've lost my mind. If I hem and haw over the question, then she's liable to storm out. Or sulk. She's liable to say I'm the most offensive, scatterbrained, illogical, indecisive and demented person who ever drew a human breath. She'll wonder aloud why she bothers to talk to me.

What I say is: talk away. I'm not listening. I'm not hearing a word you're saying.

What *are* you saying, Coolie? Lay it on me, sweetheart.

Tonight I really wasn't listening. Coolie's toenails, painted or not, lovely as they are, weren't something I felt like dwelling on. I was looking out our front window. We had the curtains

back and I was looking out there. It was dark, but I still thought
I could see him. I could see the boy out there plain as day, just
as I'd seen him earlier. This little kid. Maybe three years old.
Certainly no older than that. I had been going about the room,
straightening up things, getting rid of what Coolie calls the
clutter, and there he was. This little kid walking by. He had on
this blue sunsuit and this white shirt with a funny collar, and
these little sandals — thongs, I guess they are. They were
flip-flopping up and down and once or twice he'd lift his feet
and they'd fall off. He had on this kind of hat, but even so you
could see he had a nice head of golden hair. And this fine fair
skin. The sun was shining on him and I swear he seemed to be
glowing. He was about the prettiest kid I ever saw. But that's
not why I kept looking. He had these two adults with him,
what I would say were his parents. Nice-looking pair, young,
maybe thirty. Both had on white slacks and the man wore one
of those soft-knit shirts with an alligator over the pocket. The
woman had on this wide-brimmed hat, white, very stylish. I
wondered what they were doing strolling the sidewalk in our
neighborhood. They didn't seem to fit in. We don't get many
parents with young children out here. We don't have any
nearby schools, or day-care centers, and no playgrounds. We
got one park but the benches are all broken. No, young parents
come out here looking over the real estate, and right away they
know they want no part of it. You can't blame them. But I was
talking about that kid. The reason I was watching that kid was
because of the golf bag. It was a real one, I mean, slung over his
shoulder, about the size of a loaf of French bread. And it was a
good one, I could see that. That kid's parents were not fooling
around. This golf bag was made of finest leather, and it had
about eight to ten putts — irons, whatever they're called —
stuck in it. Protruding from the bag, you know, like a dozen
gleaming metal heads. Expensive, I could see that. Two hundred smackers, minimum, I'd say. And heavy, too, because
that little kid could hardly carry it. He kept trying to drag it

along the sidewalk, but the parents wouldn't have it. First you'd hear the father, then the mother, then the father again.

"Carry the bag," the father would say.

Then the mother: "Carry the bag, Buster. Keep it up high on your shoulder."

It took them ten minutes just to pass my house.

"Don't drag the bag, Buster."

They were pretty angry. They were trying to stay calm but you could see they wanted to swat him.

"Pick up the bag, Buster."

Finally, the kid stopped. Just stopped. You could see he didn't mean to take another step. He threw down the bag. He sailed off his hat about ten feet up the street. He gave his parents this dark look.

"What are you doing, Buster?" they said. "Come on, Buster."

"I'm golfing," he said. "Me and him are golfing." And he gave me this lidded, dark look. He'd seen me all right. He had my number. He then sorted through his clubs and took out the one he liked best. A big iron. He swung it around a time or two, getting the feel of it. His legs looked rubbery. He looked like a good breeze would send him flying. But he was cute. He was the cutest kid I ever saw. Then he got out this yellow golf ball and got out a tee and put the ball on it. The ball kept rolling off, but finally he managed. He stood up straight, on his tippy-toes, and got the club swung way back over his shoulder.

"Stand back!" he said. "Watch out!"

I had the side of my face pressed up against the window. Christ, I was barely breathing. He was really going to hit that son of a bitch. He was going to hit it hard. He was going to maul that bastard. He had his tongue between his teeth and this look of terrible wrath on his and he was going to knock holy shit out of that stupid ball.

His father rushed up and grabbed him from behind just as he was swinging. "Wait," he said. "That's not how you do it. Let me show you." And the kid was trapped. He had to do it the way his father said. "Back up. Widen your stance. Don't hold it like a baseball bat. This club isn't an ax. And your swing? Haven't I told you how to swing?"

"Listen to your father, Buster," the mother kept saying. "Listen to your father."

The kid crumpled. He just folded up. He squatted down on the sidewalk and the father had to keep yanking him up.

"Damn you, Buster!"

The kid wailed. He wailed and wailed. He squirmed and wriggled. He grabbed the ball and flung it into my hedge. He kicked at the golfing bag. He clamped his teeth into the father's arm.

The father yanked up the kid and tucked him under his arm. The kid yelled. Oh boy, how he squawled. The mother scooped up the clubs. The three of them went on out of sight. But I heard that wailing a long time. I still could.

So that's what was going through my mind as I stared out our black window. That kid. Old Buster.

"Stand back! Watch out!"

Coolie, I noticed, was giving me the once-over. She wasn't saying anything just yet, though she was looking hard. I had these two shoes I'd been shining, up in my hands. One on each hand and I figured, from the way Coolie was staring, that I must have been waving these shoes about. Slapping golf balls. Kicking at the father. I didn't know for sure, but that's what I figured.

"I worry about you," she said. "I really do. There are times, Cecil, when I know you don't have a brain in your head. You're just not all here. You're off God knows where."

She meant it, too. There was a different sound in the air. A different note struck. She'd made a new turn in the way she regarded me. What she said came from some more distant, more objective place. I even figured I knew what she was thinking: *Maybe one day we had something, this crackpot and me. Now God help us.*

That's what I figured.

So I decided I wouldn't mention just yet the lady with the money. When she came, I'd spread it out on the floor. Every dollar. Coolie could do with it whatever she wanted.

So I sat there smiling, pondering things. Considering that Saks box. Old Buster. Talking about shoes. "See these loafers," I said. "Look at these heels. It isn't healthy walking around in heels like this. What I think I'll do is go down to the shoe repair tomorrow and get me a new set put on. Maybe even throw these out, buy a new pair. What do you think?"

Coolie was eyeing me hard. Her jaw was set and she had her squint locked in; her mouth twitched; I could see her sucking in her breath. She looked old. I swear to hell she looked older than me. Yet I never felt so old as what I knew she felt, looking at me.

She wouldn't have called it age. She would have called it something that happened to us a long time ago. A decision we made.

I put the shoes down. I went over and closed the drapes.

Coolie whipped the cap over the polish bottle. No toe painting tonight.

"You are the most boring creature who ever lived," she said. "I sometimes wonder what it would be like to be you and to have your mind and to have to go through life with the mind-boggling triviality of thought that you have. How do you do it? I know these are extraordinary times and that there is no end to the bizarre, low creatures that exist on this planet, but how in God's name do you do it? In your shoes I would jump off the first cliff I came to. I would go over headfirst. As Christ is my witness, I certainly would. Now would you put away your stupid shoe stuff? Would you stop fondling that stupid Saks box? Don't leave it for me to pick up. You can go to the repair shop or go to the moon or take a flying leap, I don't care. Cecil, I really don't. First your casseroles and now your shoes. Did you think you were conducting an orchestra? You're going to drive me out of my mind, Cecil. You really are."

Old Coolie is a killer. She knows how to get you right between the eyes, when being got is the last thing you want. If you blink, there it comes again.

I threw up my hands. "I surrender," I said. "You got me cornered, officer. Just read me my rights."

She covered her face. She sat a moment on the sofa's edge, shaking her head. Moaning a little.

But she came out of it smiling. Still shaking her head, but smiling now. Old Coolie's smile knocks me out.

She padded over on her naked feet and for a second clung to me, patting my head. She worked her warm face up under my neck. "A child," she said, in a low, husky voice. "You're like a little child."

I knew that voice: Veronica Lake.

Old Coolie the sorcerer.

I gave her a tight hug. Her body stiffened and she pulled away. "Get me another beer," she said. "Another pound or two, why the Christ not!"

She flung herself down on the sofa and her fingers went *snap snap.*

"And bring it in a glass this time," she said. "I'm not an animal yet."

Ah, Coolie, you're a demon.

Coolie, sweetheart, you're a dream.

In the kitchen, opening the bottle, pouring the beer into a fake-crystal glass with a golden rim, I have these thoughts. I am thinking of that Saks box and trying to set a date for when it first showed up in the house. Five years or ten — the time flows together. It isn't my box, it isn't Coolie's, it belongs to neither of us. Maybe it was just here; maybe it goes with the house. It's just a box, goddamnit, anyway. I am looking at the leftover casserole on the table and trying to figure whether I should put it away or throw it out. I give it a sniff. It smells okay. All the right stuff has gone into it. I get out the book and flip it open to the recipe. I run a finger down what's printed there. The page is greasy and stained and it has an aroma, too. I've found a lot of goodness in that page. With minor variations, I've made this casserole a hundred times.

Maybe, I think, that's where the trouble is.

I can hear Coolie at the dining table. I can hear what Coolie is saying. What she'll say tomorrow, if I can't mend my ways. "This dish tastes like manure. This dish is horrible. But spoon me another teensy helping. I've got to eat. A person has to live."

We don't hear each other any more. I wonder why it is I am hearing that.

Habit: me with my dishes, Coolie with her words.

What I am mostly wondering about, as I stand there, is what we'd do if we had us a kid. What we would have done, way back when.

I wonder whether that kid would be like me, God help him . . . or like Coolie, God help her.

I wonder what that kid would look like.

And how old that kid would be now.

If we had us a kid I'd get that kid alone when Coolie was out of the house and I'd sit that kid down and we'd figure out a few things. We'd figure out where that Saks box came from and what came in it. We'd figure out a thousand things like that. I'd have the kid with me in the kitchen and I'd say, "Flip to page 248, kid, and let's see what goes into the old casserole tonight." And the kid would do it because me and that kid were tight as twins. The kid would slice up the onions and sauté them over a slow fire. "What next, kid?" I'd say. And the kid would dice the tomatoes and slice up the green peppers and mince a few dozen cloves of garlic. We'd pour in the olive oil. "Is that enough, kid?" I'd say, and the kid would say, "No, dad, I think that dish needs another cup or so." And I'd watch the kid pour it in. We'd stir the bastard around. I'd say, "Get me that bottle of white wine, kid," and the kid would get it and we'd smile and have us a little swig. Then before we got skunked we'd cube the shoulder of veal, forgotten until now, and we'd throw that into the skillet and brown the son of a bitch just right. We'd salt it and pepper it and butter it and I'd say, "How's that, kid?" "Just right, dad," my kid would say. "Mmmm-mmmm, I can't wait!" We'd join everything together in a big clay pot and then cover it and drop the heat to low and we'd let that bastard cook for a good two hours and fifteen minutes.

We'd stand over it, drooling.

"What's that, kid?" I'd ask. "What fine dish do we have here?"

"We have Spezzatino di Vitello," the kid would say. "We've got the best Spezzatino di Vitello any dad and his kid ever cooked up on the face of this earth."

"Bet your ass, kid," I'd say.

Then we'd light the fourteen candles and call old Coolie in. We'd install her at the table head on plump cushions and spread a lacy serviette over her lap. We'd hum her a few notes from a nice Puccini opera as we ladled up Spezzatino di Vitello on her plate. We'd click our heels as we poured her a robust wine in the table's tallest, most glittering glass.

"Eat and be merry," we'd say.

That's what we'd do, me and the kid.

I brought in Coolie her glass of beer, pulling up the side table so she could get at it without disturbing herself. She was stretched out on the sofa with one pillow over her face and another tucked between her legs.

"I would have ordered it from China," she said, "if I had known you were going to take all day. What in the name of God were you doing back there?"

Having me a kid, I thought to say. But I stayed quiet. All hell would break loose if I said that. Coolie would fly up screeching. She'd come at me like a bat out to suck blood. To suck it and ladle it on her nails. Songbird Red.

Coolie sipped at her beer. "It's not cold," she said. "It's gone flat."

I turned on a lamp or two.

"But far be it from me to complain," she said. "That's right. Run up the bills."

I tried my loafers out. Tested the shine. They were buffed up to a nice gleam all around. They looked pretty good, although my heels sank down into the floor. It was like walking on eggs, kind of curvy, I mean. I wondered how I'd ever let them get run-down like that.

I rolled the TV up, got it going, then settled down into my chair.

"I'm not watching that junk," Coolie said.

I got up and turned the TV off. It made a sizzling sound, like fat in a frying pan. It always does. That TV, I thought, it's got a mind of its own.

Coolie took the pillow off her face and jammed it under her head. I watched her toes go through their ABCs.

"Last night," she said. "Where did you go last night?"

"Bowling," I said.

She snatched herself up, glaring. "You son of a bitch," she said. "You haven't been bowling in twenty years."

Old Coolie: I find nothing in life so buoyant to me as her abuse.

Something else got her attention. She leaped up and stalked over to the wall. She stayed there the longest time, gravely studying the floor, one hand under her chin.

"You missed a spot," she said. "Did the vacuum break down? You missed this whole area."

I don't hear you, I thought. Coolie, I don't hear a word you're saying.

"Come here," she said.

I went over.

She pointed.

"That's dirt," she said. "Now that is what I call genuine dirt. That's *dirt*, Cecil. Were you planning on putting in a field of corn?"

I laughed. Old Coolie and her corn: to hear her tell it I've put in a thousand acres in the living room alone. I started off after the vacuum. Coolie brushed by me, racing fast. "No, no," she said, "don't tax yourself. I know some things are just beyond you."

She wrestled out the vacuum and got the spot cleaned to her satisfaction. But her gown got caught in the suction — she shrieked. It was nearly ripped off her.

"It's trying to tell you something, Coolie," I said. "It's maybe telling you that gown needs a little attention."

This remark went past her. But it gave me this little idea. I figured that tomorrow while she was out at work I'd soak it in the Ivory Snow. I'd soak it for about nine hours.

"You're right about that floor," I said. "Heck, I can see the difference. Heck, a person could eat off it now."

"*You* eat off it, Cecil. Not me."

"Spezzatino di Vitello," I said. "A fine floor dish."

She ignored this. She flung herself down on the sofa, groaned, then leaped up again. She got the TV going. "Anything is better than your company," she said. "I'm worn out, just knowing you're here."

I put her nail polish away, up on the mantel where she keeps it, behind the brass deer.

I put the cowboy boots back in the closet.

I gathered up the shoe-polish stuff and put it into the Saks box and stored it away.

Saks, it said. Saks Fifth Avenue. It said this on the top and on all four sides, in a nice black script. Flaring across, black on white. Pretty sharp. But where did we get it? When? What had come in this box?

"Now, kid," I said, "this one is for you to figure out. You get no sleep tonight until you figure it out."

"Okay, dad."

I must have said this aloud, or something like it, for Coolie was calling me. She had her "yell" button pushed. You'd have thought she'd just busted her kneecap up against a fire hydrant.

"You silly old bastard," she said. "What are you doing? Why are you in there mumbling to yourself? I thought someone was with you. Get in here. There's a movie on."

I came back in smiling, and took my chair.

The old TV music was getting zippy. It was really going.

"Look at that!" Coolie said, bolting up. "Can you believe it? What rubbish!"

It was some guy up in an old two-seater, two-engine plane, in pretty bad weather. In black and white this one was — how I like it best. This guy was out on wet storm-tossed wing, slipping and sliding. Squirming along. Dana Andrews it was. Dana? I wasn't sure. He looked a bit like Dana. Fog or clouds — this white stuff — kept swirling across his face. But getting blacker all the time. Whoever he was, he meant business. He wasn't out for a Sunday stroll. He was up to something, out on that wing. *Zap! Zap!* Lightning was flashing all across the sky. Jagged, bristling bolts. *Crack!* Another one. There went a propeller. The camera came in on this guy's face — it wasn't Dana, too bad — and you could see he was worried. He was desperate. But squirming along. Then we got another shot. He had this knife sticking out of his back. A delicate — what I would say was definitely a feminine — item. That knife. Pearl handle. Oodles of blood.

When the wings tilted you could see the raging sea, and swollen ice caps beyond.

"Oh God!" cried Coolie, slapping her head. "I can't believe this! Who do they think we are!"

The old music was really waltzing; it was jitterbugging to beat the band.

The man on the wing was shouting at someone as he

crawled. You couldn't hear what he was saying. The wind just whistled it away. It doesn't matter. People don't hear you anyway. We heard something though. Yep. There it went. That old prop. It ripped away and plunged whining into the sea.

Coolie was twisting about. Shrieking. She had herself tied up in knots. "Get on with it, man! Shake that load out of your britches."

I kept getting a glimpse of this white hand at the bottom of the screen.

Coolie kicked her foot out at the man. At Dana. Maybe it was Dana. He had Dana's lips. That way of measuring things.

"Will he save her?" Coolie asked. "Christ, this is a new low even for them!"

Save what *her*, I wondered. Save *who*?

Oh. That hand.

My mind was drifting a bit. The "Pick Pix of the Week" was sailing by me. Hold the phone, I was thinking. Hold that phone. Because I was thinking of that kid. My kitchen ace. Of kids, with maybe that Saks box thrown in. What if we had us *two* kids living here, I thought. A boy and a girl. Say we had a girl to match up with my kitchen ace. Brother and sister. Say that girl kid was named...well, what? There is Louise, after my mother. Louise Proffit. Now that's not bad. A girl can get along with a calling card like that. Or Celeste. Suppose we call her Celeste. Or Cynthia. How about Cynthia? Clea? Clea would be all right. That's a thought. Nothing wrong with Clea. Wait a minute though. Hold the phone. Clea Proffit? That's no good. What that is is a joke. Clear profit, get it? Actually, it isn't that bad. It's joky, but has a certain style. Class. Clea Proffit, attorney-at-law. Clea Proffit, brain surgeon. Something like that. Secretary-general, United Nations. Heck, she'd be about twelve now, old Clea would. Maybe the oldest. Say she's the oldest. Though she still sucks her thumb. Probably always will. Who cares. Clea, darling, you can suck your thumb.

"All right, daddy."

Christ yes, I was really getting into it. I could *hear* old Clea.
"Whatever you say, daddy."

Beautiful voice. Clea Proffit, star of stage and screen.

All right, this is how it is. This is how it would be. While the
kid and me are out in the kitchen getting a bead on dinner,
sipping the wine, talking about that box, Clea is in here
keeping Coolie company. Talking away. Having a fine chat.
Neither hearing the other, of course, but...well, she'd have
nice long hair, Clea would, maybe golden like that boy with the
golf clubs. A perky little nose. Beautiful eyes, a lively face.
Creamy complexion. Bit of a mess around the lips just now
because she's been out in the kitchen checking out our dish.
Saying "Ummmm good!" Now she's in here. Chatting. Smart
as a whip. "Too many missiles, mama. Too many warheads.
Stamp out the warheads." Coolie's plaiting her hair. Yes.
Talking shop. "No, no, mama. Allende was a *good* man. He
was a *good* man." Pretty but not too pretty. She'd have my
looks and Coolie's character. She'd have Coolie's screech if ever
something riled her. "No, no, mama. The Tomb of the
Unknown is a *symbol*; it isn't a Communist plot." Good at her
books. No trouble to anyone. A free spirit. She'd have friends,
about a hundred. They'd always be over, smushing the cushions,
emptying the fridge. Playing records. Whispering, giggling.
She'd have this best friend, a wee, waifish, reddish-haired
creature named Prissy. No, named Scarlet. She and that Scarlet
kid would be always together. Chattering away, not hearing
each other. "No, no, Scarlet. Turkey *claims* Cyprus. That's
where they are trying to stamp out the Kurds." But they'd
hear me and my kitchen ace when we called them in to dinner.

"Soup's on! Come get your Spezzatino di Vitello!"

And Coolie would roar: "Not *again*! I *hate* Spezzatino di
Vitello! I can't *stand* Spezzatino di Vitello! Spezzatino makes
me *sick*!"

But my daughter and little Scarlet would go to her. They'd
bring her around. They'd say, "Yes, you do, mama. Yes you

do. You know you love Spezzatino di Vitello. We all do. Our Spezzatino is delicious.''

"I know,'' Coolie would whisper. "I adore it. I just can't admit it to *him*.''

That's what I was thinking as I watched the black and white. These were bad thoughts. Depressing thoughts. I hadn't had thoughts like this in a month of Sundays — which isn't so long, now I think of it.

"Are you listening, Cecil!'' Coolie cried. "Are you *alert* to this! Can you believe it!''

The music thundered.

The plane was burning.

One wing had fallen off.

A girl was dangling in the sky. The man was holding her by one arm. His grip slipping inch by inch. The poor girl was weeping. Weeping and screeching. She reminded me of Coolie. Coolie, too, was accustomed to seeing life from this woman's point of view. You could see sharks circling in the water below. Lightning flashing. The careening plane a black line of smoke. The girl in the sky, wriggling. She was terrified. The wind throwing her about. She had on this flimsy dress that looked a bit like Coolie's gown. Flapping about. Shredding. Now and then the music would drop so you could hear their speech. Their gasps. Their hard breath. The lick of flames fast approaching. Hold on, the man kept saying. Hold tight. The girl was getting more naked by the minute. Pretty soon we were going to have us an X-rated movie. She was trying to tell him something, though you couldn't make it out. The music boomed in each time we went to her. But she seemed to be saying something about that knife. Yes, the knife, for the camera kept swaying to the knife in old Dana's back. "Forgive me,'' she was saying. "Forgive me, my lover, my pet. My lamb.''

Coolie, I forgive you.

Coolie, you set my heart a-racing.

Coolie, let's climb into bed.

"Hush up," said Coolie. "Be quiet. I'm listening to this."

The other wing fell off.

The fuselage cracked in half.

The music crashed in. The scene faded to black.

"Jesus help us," said Coolie in a moan. She was wrenching about on the sofa, her eyes closed, a pillow clenched under her chin. Old Coolie loves her movies. "What's the point!" she yelled to the TV. "Jesus, I hate these miserable endings. Do they live or die? Are you morons? Do you think *we* are?"

Just then I heard the door bell ring. Coolie didn't notice. She had her hands up over her ears now, watching the quivering screen.

Bing-pong! — there went the bell again. I took the time to check myself in the mirror. I smoothed back my hair. Put on my polished shoes.

I walked on out to the front door and swung it open.

She was dressed in a belted coat so immaculate it seemed to shimmer, and sheer white stockings the same color, and I never got to notice her shoes because she was speaking to me, her hair swept back on both sides and her face so pale, white, and clean she looked the twin of her pristine garments.

"It's all here," she said, "every last penny. I'm glad you let me bring it out this evening. I tell you, it will be a load off my mind, getting rid of this money. We don't usually handle so much."

She had a nice voice, on the soft side. Silver earrings gleamed from her lobes and there was a silk scarf, not exactly white, circling her throat. She was about my height and her hair had a reddish tinge. She had this fine leather satchel strapped to one arm.

She was younger than I had figured.

She had a sweet shape.

An easy, comfortable way of looking you in the eye.

"No trouble I hope," I said. "I wouldn't want you to go to any extra trouble on my account."

"No trouble at all," she said.

I asked if she wanted to come inside. Maybe take off that coat, meet the wife, have a quiet chat. She said no. No, she had to run. She had plans, she said. The evening was still young.

I peeked around her. There was a small shiny car by the curb, with someone sitting in it.

"Do you want to count it?" she said.

I told her no, no point in that.

I took the satchel.

"Do I have to sign for it?" I asked. "The old John Henry? Are there any strings attached? Is there anything I ought to know about this money?"

"No," she said. "It's yours. It's yours and that's all there is to it."

She was a nice girl with a nice sweet voice and she had these remarkable eyes, clear as rainwater.

I had no trouble hearing her.

"We were wondering," she said — hesitating, not wanting to pry — "we were wondering what you intend doing with it."

"Do with it?" I said. "I don't know."

"Well...good night then."

"There's this kid," I said. "Down in Nigeria."

"Oh yes?"

"He's been getting fifty cents a week. I've been sending him that much. Now I might raise it to a dollar."

"We hoped you'd do something like that," she said.

She was turning to go. She had this handbag strapped over her shoulder, not white exactly but more the color of that scarf, and she was digging into it. She brought out a pair of high heels.

"Do you figure a dollar is enough?" I asked.

She slowed her steps. I could see her mulling this over. Fifty cents or a dollar — it was an important question.

"I *suppose* so," she said. "You have to keep these things in proportion."

I could see that little kid with his hand out, stretching all across the continent. Those big eyes. The scabs. The spindly legs. Named Lopé, I think. Lopé something-or-other. Something like that.

Lopé Proffit. It killed me every time I thought of that kid.

"Hell," I said, "I might make it *two* dollars! What the hell."

She leaned up against the porch post, taking off her low business heels and sliding the new ones on. Then she pitched the lows into her handbag and snapped it shut.

"Wait a minute," I said. "There's another one down in Peru. Peru, of all places. Can you beat that? A little girl this one is. Pathetic-looking, but the energy she has! These stick legs, sores all over her body — pus! — and her feet turned in so you know she'll never be much of a runner. Never a golfer. Millet and rice, that's what she eats. Not much of that, either. The flies! She's got a thousand flies buzzing all over. On her mouth too, feeding on those sores. Giving itch to the scabs. Lice in her hair. But what stamina! Christ, my heart bleeds. Marjula her name is. Marjula, what kind of name is that? But I like it. Christ, Marjula is plenty good enough for me. Hard *h*, you get it? Hula, a real hula girl. Take ten of our kids over here just to hold her down, and I'm including that kid with the golf clubs and the golden hair. 'Watch out! Stand back! Don't get in my way!' That's what old Marjula is always saying. It's the message I get. What do you think? Am I on the right track? I think five dollars a week myself. Five, just until she learns how to count. Maybe hook her up with that Nigeria fella. Get something going. Lopé and Marjula. What do you think? I could call it my 'Green-Light Special,' what's coming at them this week from our neck of the woods. Would that knock out her eyes? Shoo away them flies? An orphan, you know. No mama, no daddy. Scabby like him. Big protruding belly. But she's ours now, old Coolie's and mine. Did I say five? Forget five. I say ten, minimum, and that's cheap, my bargain this week. Am I on the right track? Am I talking sense?"

She had got down the steps and out onto the walk. She

looked pretty sharp in her high heels. She was a pretty handsome woman, what you'd call a bit of all right.

"It's a question of their *perspective*," she said. "You can't raise false expectations. That would never do."

This baffled me. I wondered how it was she thought any of us lived. How any of us had survived.

"Clear up the drinking water," I said. "Buy *real* milk. Speed that up. Hey, I got it. Another water buffalo!"

She laughed. It was a good, high, hard laugh, lots of enjoyment in it. I forgave her all her sins.

"I hear you," she said. "You're coming in loud and clear. It's your money. All yours. Ta ta."

She went on down the path, that coat shimmering. It was nicely cut, that coat, beautifully form fitting. She had wonderful legs, a strong stride.

"Going dancing?" I said.

She swirled. She gave a little rat-tat-tat to the pavement. "You bet!" she said. "All night long!"

The man in the car grinned and waved.

"So long."

I walked into the living room with the satchel of money.

"It isn't over," Coolie said without turning around.

She meant the movie. The man from the airplane and the woman in the tattered dress were up in the Andes somewhere. Snow all over. I wondered how they had survived the crash. But I granted them that. Funny things happen in this world.

"Where've you been?" Coolie said. "You missed the best part."

These two were hugging each other. Trembling. They looked pretty beaten. It was cold up there. The highest peak, old Clea would say, this side of Asia. Snow swirling every which way. They were trying to talk but their teeth were chattering too hard.

"She's his wife," Coolie said.

Now they were trying to get a fire going. They scooped out a deep hole in the snow. They scratched up a few twigs. They crouched down inside the hole. He got out his matches. They studied each other over the flame. They got this dark, serious look in their eyes. You could see it happening: the desire swelling up. The music, too. They were crying. Suddenly they slammed into each other, moaning and twisting, driving at each other's lips and throat, as the snow dropped over them like huge wafers. The matches got kicked over with snow. They got kicked farther. Not that this pair noticed or cared. They were going at it. You can't say no to such desire. You can't say no, I guess, whether you're in the Andes, at the Proffit house, or on a bridge in Venice.

Coolie didn't agree. Her face was up at the screen. She was shaking her fists and yelling at them. "Build the fire!" she said. "Oh, you suckers, build the fire! You'll die, damn you!"

Snow blanketed the screen. You could just peer through it to see that human beings were there.

"They won't die, Coolie," I said. "It's only a movie."

I started spreading the money out over the carpet.

I started counting the money.

The Madwoman of Cherry Vale

RIPLEY'S DAY BEGAN without complications. He stirred at seven when his wife Esther arose, and thereafter floated about between sleep and dim wakefulness as she went through her usual morning routine. He heard the shower running, and then didn't; he heard the hair dryer going, heard the odd little clatter of bottles, the tinkle of jewelry, the soft slide of drawers. Heard her exasperation when she drew on stockings that had a run. "Helpless, it's helpless," he heard her say. He opened his eyes once, to look at the clock, and caught a glimpse of Esther in the FloatAway mirror doors, sliding a silk dress over her head. The yellow rectangle of light filling the doorway was comforting to him. The sky, too, he saw without lifting his head, was streaked with gold. Nice weather, for a change. He rolled to his side, away from the light. And dozed, fading into and out of tranquil dream. Then she'd turned off the light, approached the bedside, and was kissing him. He murmured a greeting and she went on downstairs.

So far, so good.

These early morning sleeps were precious to him. Bliss, he thought. Bliss is what I feel.

But this morning Esther had walked into the kitchen and screamed. "Ripley, Ripley!" she'd called — "come here!" That and no more. Or no more that he heard. Nothing that conveyed any further emergency, or explained *why* he should

146

come down now. He had only fifteen minutes or so before he too had to get up, and though her calling him, her screeching, was irregular, he thought no more about it because once again he'd fallen deeply asleep. He came out of it a few other times, to hear her distraught yells, her calling his name, but he'd pulled the covers over his head and stayed on.

So when at seven-thirty he got up, slipped his robe on, washed his face and brushed his teeth and padded barefoot into the kitchen, he was unprepared for what was there to greet him: not his wife at all, no sign of her, but a woman he'd never seen.

She was seated at the white wrought-iron table in the sunroom off the kitchen, sipping from a mug — *his* mug — her elbows resting on the green glass top.

"Good morning," she said smiling. "I can see *you* rested well. Have a seat then, the coffee's hot."

And she was already rising, asking what he'd like for breakfast, and giving every indication that she meant to make it for him herself.

He remembered his wife's shouts, but was not alarmed. Although it was odd to find a stranger in the house, he assumed she was some friend whom Esther had an urgent need to see, despite the early hour. Esther had numerous activities, numerous acquaintances, and there had been little time lately to sort them out.

"Where's Esther?" he asked.

But the woman, stooped at the open refrigerator, hands straight against her knees, apparently didn't hear.

He sat a moment, still a bit befuddled with sleep, thinking he would first have shaved had he known a visitor was in the house. He sipped his coffee and tried not to make his stares at the woman too blatant.

"Who are you?" he finally said. "My name's Ripley." He smiled cheerfully, wanting to let the woman know that any friend of his wife's was welcome, whatever the time. Although it was a little embarrassing to be sitting here in his robe and bare feet, feeling naked, and a bit like an intruder in his own house.

The woman's response puzzled him.

"Oh you know me, Ripley. I'm Agnes!"

And she got the eggs and butter and slammed open a few cabinet doors, presumably looking for a frying pan, since that eventually was what she came up with.

She set it on the stove and unwrapped the butter.

"Fried, this morning?" she said. "Or scrambled? I can do them that nice double-boiler method, if you like. Would you like bacon also?"

"No," he said. "Listen, I can really do this myself."

But she got out bacon anyway and separated the slices and spread them evenly in the pan.

Ripley got up and went about the house. He called his wife's name in a low voice, but she didn't reply and he didn't come across her. He looked for a note at the secretary, her favorite place for leaving them, but found nothing. He even went down into the basement, where it was most unlikely Esther would have gone. He stepped out into the yard and looked around. He went to the garage. Her car was still there. So was his.

"Where is Esther?" he said, returning to the kitchen.

The woman standing at the stove, spatula in hand, turned to him with an agreeable smile. She had set the table properly, using their best china. She had washed out his mug and it was now in place, filled with steaming coffee. She'd found a single rose, from God knows where, and had it centered in a tulip vase. "I don't know," she said. "She was here one minute and the next she was gone. She called your name. I expect you heard her. We got in a bit of a flap over that. I told her she should let you sleep, that you probably needed it. Then we talked a while. She seemed nervous and quite upset. Then she went out the back door without a word, and I haven't seen her since."

"Good lord!" said Ripley. "What on earth can be wrong? It's not like her at all."

"I should hope not," said the woman. "She was very nearly rude. You'd have thought she hated me. I can't imagine why."

"You have business with her, I take it."

"Not so much that. No, nothing unusual. I was simply here trying to answer her questions as best I could, and suddenly, after you didn't come down, she let out a curse, said, 'Well, I'm not standing for this!' — and went away. I couldn't say what was the matter."

"But she didn't take her car!" Ripley said.

The woman shrugged.

Ripley prowled the floor a bit, shaking his head. He couldn't figure it out. Esther wasn't given to unreasonable tantrums. She led a hectic, but rigorous and orderly existence.

The woman served the breakfast, including a plate for herself, and they sat opposite each other, not saying much. He was hungrier than he had supposed. The eggs, done the double-boiler way, were buttery and delicious. Left to his own devices, on mornings when there was time, he prepared them this way himself, although it was a waste. Esther rarely breakfasted. She had her coffee au-lait style, and perhaps might nibble at an edge of toast.

It delighted him that this woman's appetite was the match of his own.

His gaze went time and time again to the flower. That, too, delighted him. Such a nice touch. But it was hardly the season; where the hell had she got it?

When he looked at her she smiled in a friendly way, and when he wasn't looking at her he was aware that she was either closely regarding him, or looking about the room, into all its corners, and through the windows at the garden and untended ground beyond, as if to set all such arrangements in her head. She didn't talk a great deal; he was happy about that. Esther was inclined to run on and on.

"You must have got here very early this morning," he said. It had occurred to him that he'd seen no car belonging to her. Someone must have dropped her off. But her answer astonished him.

"Oh no!" she exclaimed. "I spent the night."

"Where?" he blurted out.

"In the guest room. I was quite comfortable. Thank you," she said.

Ripley wondered why his wife had not told him they had a guest in. He wondered — and studied her secretly for some sign — what the guest had made of their behavior last night. He and Esther had gone through a couple of bottles of champagne. They'd sat laughing, poking the fire. They'd danced naked on the living-room carpet and played loud music. They'd necked on the sofa.

It was incredible, he thought, that Esther had let him go through that entire evening of frolic without mentioning the presence of a guest.

What *is* going on? he thought. I've underestimated Esther. She's clearly up to something.

His wife still hadn't showed up half an hour later when he stood at the door, explaining to the stranger that he had to go off to work. He had a train to catch. He'd be gone all day. Could he drop her in town?

"Oh no," she said. "I'll stay here!"

He fidgeted, hesitating. He told himself he wasn't really worried. Esther would surely be back soon and in any case this stranger must be a very good friend of hers or she would never have disappeared, leaving matters this way. Some of Esther's friends *looked* freaky, but they were all pretty much on the up-and-up. Agnes hardly seemed the sort who would strip the house of its heirlooms.

"All right," he said. "Make yourself at home."

She showed marvellous teeth as she laughed, and even

whirled around on one foot. She seemed to find this remark hilarious.

"I *am* home!" she said.

Driving into the station, he figured it out. The visitor was some kind of relative of Esther's. But why had she never mentioned this odd, rather pretty, totally agreeable woman? Why? Well, that was easy. Both this one *and* Esther had their odd side. Probably — well, clearly — they didn't get along.

But when had the woman come *into* the house? Last night he and Esther had dined at home; they'd been in all evening and had had no callers. Had she entered while he was down in the cellar getting the champagne? Then why hadn't she joined them for at least one drink?

Puzzling. Really puzzling.

Ripley mentioned the experience to his friend Joe Ortman, who sat beside him on the train.

"Nothing weird about it," said Ortman. "I'm always at my house finding people underfoot I never saw before. People I don't know from Adam. Even their animals. I swear we had one kid come in for three weeks, he had these two big lumbering black beasts with him, Alsatians, I guess they were. Are Alsatians black? Anyway, they were the biggest mothers you ever saw, ate tons of food, and chewed on whatever got put in front of them: me, the sofas, the drapes. He'd sneak them upstairs to his room at night after we'd gone to bed. Sneak in my daughter too, for all I know. She's the one always bringing these clowns home. 'We're not serious,' she says, 'just thinking about it.' Cracks me up, the times I've heard her say that. What I've noticed is that they all have huge appetites and don't mind rifling the liquor cabinet. I've seen my own suit, tie, and shoes coming at me a hundred times. I tell you it's terrible being wealthy, this day and age. Sometimes I think my daughter was dropped in a basket at my doorstep by some goddamned socialist, or Communist, or worse. No, I wouldn't worry about your visitor. She sounds harmless enough. I wouldn't worry about Esther either. I've never seen that lady when her hands were tied."

Ripley looked out the train's moving window. The sky had clouded up.

"Looks like rain," he said.

"Shit," said Ortman. "Only yesterday some asshole walked off with my raincoat."

Upon arriving at his office, Ripley called home.

"No," Agnes told him. "She's not showed up yet."

He held the phone between chin and shoulder, doodling on his desk pad, trying to think of some way of holding her on the line, wanting to ask her what she'd been doing with herself but unable quite to do it without seeming to question her right to be there. He imagined her shifting through desk drawers, reading love letters, examining his bank account.

She apparently sensed something of this. "I've cleaned our dishes," she said. "Dusted some. I don't mean to criticize your wife, but the kitchen shelves really were a horror."

"Christ," he said, irritated. "You don't need to mess about with crap like that!"

"I like it," she said. She was silent a moment, then added: "I've made our beds. I've put your green robe in the tub to soak with a little Zero. It *is* washable, I read the label." She was silent again.

He could see the green robe in the sudsy tub. But he couldn't see whether it was in the upstairs tub or in the downstairs one off the guest room. He had a suspicion, without knowing why, that it would be the latter.

"Shall I do the laundry?" she said. "I couldn't help noticing oodles and oodles stacked up in the laundry room."

He stared at the phone. Was the woman demented?

"Pretty stinky," she said.

He laughed. That was precisely why he and Esther avoided the room until they could put the wash off no longer.

"Don't touch it," he said. "Sit down and read a book. Esther would slice my throat if she knew I let you do any of that crap."

"I was thinking of taking a drive," she said. "I found your wife's keys on the sideboard."

Ripley said nothing.

"I'm a perfectly safe driver," she said. "I drive defensively."

He could hear her laughing at herself.

"But I won't do it if you think you wife would mind. I know how sensitive some people are about their property."

He wondered why she never called Esther by name. Christ, they must have had quite a row this morning.

But if that was the case, why was she hanging around?

"Maybe I won't take that drive," he heard her say. Then she hung up. She sounded hurt.

He worked for an hour or so, initialing this form and that, shoving papers about, routing reports and recommendations and statistics and sales graphs to one department or another. Esther hated his job. A thousand times he'd heard her say that if she had his job to do one day she'd puncture her lung with an ice pick.

"You should be tooting around in sports cars, talking money out of old widows," she said, "who would hand over a fortune for each one of your smiles."

She'd say: "You should be doing something dramatic, for Christ's sake."

Yes, Esther couldn't abide anything that smelled of the treadmill. She loved money, but deplored the regularity of paychecks.

"Each Friday every second week? Christ, why don't you go in and snatch it up on a Thursday? Next time tell them you want it all in dimes. I'd as soon be kissed by a dead man as lead the life you lead."

Where *was* Esther? Why didn't she *call*? Didn't she know he'd be worried about her?

He reviewed his time in bed that morning. *"Helpless, it's*

helpless.'' He remembered her saying that. Was she betraying some deep psychological state, expressing her passage through some point of no return? Was she saying their marriage was finished? Or was she speaking only of the run in her stockings? But she'd kissed him. She'd said good morning. Her actions had been perfectly routine, following a wonderful night. Until she'd gone downstairs. Her screech: *"Ripley, come here!"* A genuinely authentic screech, brought about because something or someone had surprised, perhaps alarmed her. Agnes? But Agnes was straight as a row of beans. And not nearly the physical match of Esther. Esther was taller, wider, sturdier — had a lot more muscle. Agnes was smallish, pale, quiet; she looked a little sickly, in fact. As if she'd been encarcerated for a long time in a place where sunlight was restricted, rationed out. No, Agnes would not set Esther's teeth on edge. Agnes she could handle. What then? Had they concocted this together? Their idea of a good joke to play on him? Or had she summoned him this morning out of genuine need and then, as he didn't respond, had she said to hell with him and stormed out the door?

Or — possibly this — was he over-responding?

If he called the police, the police would surely laugh. Scarcely three hours had gone by.

"Foul play, mister? You must be nuts."

Yet he couldn't shake the feeling — the possibility — that something dreadful had happened to her. She liked drama, Esther did, but she would never inflict unnecessary pain. She loved writing notes, telephoning, checking in.

It was out of character, damnit. It made no sense.

Before noon, he called home again. This time, too, Agnes answered, racing, obviously out of breath. Where had his call found her? In the garden, turning sod? Down in the basement, dismembering Esther's body, stacking it in the deep freeze?

He shivered, concentrating on what Agnes was saying: "No,

not a word.... Yes, it's very strange.... No, I have no explanation whatsoever." He asked if she and Esther were — he hesitated, searching for the right phrase — "what you would call good friends?"

Agnes hesitated, too.

"I don't know," she said. "More or less. We're...what might be termed cold-weather friends."

Ripley was at a loss. He had no idea what Agnes was intending to convey.

"You say she was pretty strung out this morning when she left?"

"She was in a rage. At you, I think. At me, too, but mostly at you. I've tried figuring it out, but can't."

"Excuse me for prying," Ripley said, "but what business did you have with Esther this morning?"

He heard the clunk of the phone. For a moment he thought they had been disconnected.

"I can't reveal that," she said.

"It's too personal?"

"Well, yes...too personal, but mostly too embarrassing."

"I see."

"For all of us."

"All of us?"

"I can say this. We talked about you. Yes, your name came up more than once."

He frowned. He wondered if this Agnes didn't have a screw loose somewhere. She sounded pathetic and childish and more than a little foggy.

"What about me?"

"Oh, you know. In a general way."

He persisted, but she would say no more. She seemed to want mostly to talk about his bathrobe.

"I stretched it out to dry on the floor over towels," she said. "It's very heavy material, though, and I don't think it will be dry for several days. I noticed you have another in your closet.

That Oriental-type thing? I hope you won't mind wearing it until the other is ready."

He refused to discuss this with her. He said good-bye, and hung up.

Christ, she was sounding exactly like someone's idea of an old-fashioned wife. It wouldn't surprise him if she rang up and asked that he bring home pork chops for dinner. A weird one, he thought. Where the hell did Esther find her?

He had his secretary get the number of Violet Witherspoon, reputedly Esther's best friend.

At his explanation, Violet laughed. "I played tennis with her yesterday," she said. "We had a few drinks. She said she was going home and ravage you....Did she? Good....No, I've never heard her mention anyone named Agnes. Agnes *who*?... Said nothing to me about a guest."

Violet wasn't worried. That was a relief.

"She's probably walking to Memphis," she said. "Esther has always been saying she was going to get out on the highway one day and walk a thousand miles. Don't worry, Ripley. Your honey will come back to you."

After hanging up, he too thought it lame of him not to have got from Agnes her last name. He called home instantly.

"How sweet of you," Agnes said.

"Pardon?"

"To keep calling me. I'm quite enjoying it."

She didn't appear to take in that it was Esther about whom he was concerned.

"Matter of curiosity," Ripley told her, "but what is your surname? I'm afraid I missed it this morning."

There was a shocked silence, then Agnes's rich laughter over the wire.

"Don't be silly!" she said. "James!" she said. "*James*! The same as yours."

He pretended to laugh with her.

"What a coincidence," he said. "Still, there are lots of Jameses in this neck of the woods."

She said a slow yes. She seemed not quite to grasp his point.

"Not an uncommon name," he said.

She went right on laughing. "What has *that* got to do with it?"

He was thoroughly confused.

"Ripley?" she said.

"Yes?"

"Shall I make the dinner? Shall I have it ready for eightish or so? We'll have cocktails before, if you like."

He hung up in a flurry of consternation and worry. Apparently Agnes meant to hang around a bit. He wished he had his wife there to explain. He wondered where she was. He wondered why this was happening to him.

His secretary chose that moment to sweep in. She announced she was going to lunch. "You'll mind the phone," she said. They eyed each other. Gloria Phelan, for reasons not clear to either of them, did not like him. He'd once overheard her telling another woman that he was "namby-pamby" and "wishy-washy" and had "no taste." Gloria was wearing her destructive outfit today, a scarlet usherette's suit with a flaring black scarf. Her hair was cut in a punkish way, with green swipes over each ear. Her lipstick was the color of chocolate pudding. A triangle was painted on her left cheek.

"Sit down, Miss Phelan," he said. "Will you?"

"Be brief," she said. She sat. He began pacing. What he hoped to do was to lay the bare bones of his situation before Gloria Phelan, and get from her an objective point of view. He bungled it, however:

"Miss Phelan," he said, "what would you say if I told you that since last night there has been a strange woman living in my house, and that since this morning my wife has disappeared?"

Miss Phelan was already standing. She strode to the door.

"Mr. James," she said. "What you do in the privacy of your own environment is no concern of mine. All I ask is that you not involve *me*. Is that clear? I do not appreciate this conversation."

He was about to protest, but the woman, after a piteous glance at him, hastened away. The phone rang. He leaped to it.

It was Ortman, of all people.

"Didn't tell you about that one who set fire to the swimming pool," Ortman said. "He drove for this oil company. One night he emptied the truck in my pool. Then threw a match into it. You probably read about it. Hell, it was a five-alarmer. The city tried billing *me*, for Christ's sake."

Ortman told a few other stories about his daughter's beaux. Then he said: "Look out your window. Is it still raining?" Ripley said yes it was, and Ortman, cursing, hung up.

Ortman wants to be my pal, Ripley thought. Yet I don't cotton much to him.

He sat out at his secretary's desk until she returned — with withering looks, her complexion dark as a smoked eel.

"You misunderstood me, Miss Phelen."

"You're in my seat," she said. "Kindly scratch ass."

He brooded over Esther's absence at lunch and at work that afternoon could get little accomplished. He wanted to go home, find her address book, start calling people. He dialed Violet Witherspoon again, but Violet was out. Who else was Esther chummy with? First names came to him — Rory, Phyllis, Gladys, Heather — but nothing else. There were scores of such women in and out of the house, calling in the evening for long, sometimes whispered, chats. Grace and Slick and Bonnie. Isola, there was one. Isola *who*? Bonnie *what*? Last week there had been an exercise class with Violet and who else? Bev. Bea. No, with Vee Beaverdeck, said to have the most fabulous shape.

He had his secretary get the Beaverdeck number. He called, explained. The man to whom he spoke sounded guarded. More than guarded. He sounded deranged. "What is this?" he kept saying. "What's going on? Why bother me? There ain't no Esther here. Vee's gone. What are you saying, man? Get off my back. I got my own troubles too, you know."

At four Ripley packed his case and called it a day. He caught the early train home. As the cars swept into one station after another, he watched the doors, fully expecting to see Esther barrel in, one among a pack of women somewhat like herself. They'd be carrying shopping bags, giant boxes, pandas the size of loop-o-planes. They'd be swinging golf clubs, lurching down the aisle, dropping their goods, bumping people, demanding seats. Was that how Esther would have spent her day? Or would she have been at this or that *kaffee klatsch*, setting up committees to defend seals, to protest armaments and radium poisoning or the wanton murder of whales? He didn't know. He had no idea.

This was true, however: her life was more interesting than his. *"Ripley, come here!"* She was more responsible on all fronts; had he called her name, in a moment of panic or fear, she'd have been Johnny-on-the-spot. She would have stormed forth, ready to slay all dragons. She would have rescued him.

"I miss her," he said aloud. "I've got to have her back." He felt like crying. Had he been out in the woods, or alone on a desert range, he'd have bayed like a dog.

A woman seated forward caught his eye. She wore a checkered coat, a checkered hat and gloves, a zebra purse. He wished that woman were Esther. He wanted to move toward her and hug her and settle his face against her neck. The woman snapped open her purse and withdrew from it a compact encased in imitation zebra fur. She opened it in front of her face and floated her head from side to side, examining her teeth.

She was in her sixties, now scowling his way, a tank. Her swollen ankles were crossed, and tucked up under the seat, as if they did not belong to her.

"People staring," he heard her say. "It's disgusting, you want to know the truth."

Several heads nodded, and stared at him.

My wife has disappeared, he wanted to tell them. I've got a strange woman staying at my house.

Joe Ortman had told a lie about that swimming-pool caper. No one had set fire to his pool. He'd have read about it in the paper or heard it talked about at parties. Esther would have said Joe Ortman was a pill and deserved whatever trouble came his way.

The train curved into the station. People were rising to disembark.

There was no rain now. It had got colder.

On the drive home, gearing up to a mile or so above the limit and then slowing because a cop car had tucked in behind him, he dwelled a moment on the fat woman and what Esther's mother called her daughter's conservative streak. Esther hated checks. "Cardboard salesmen wear checks," she said. "And cardboard salesmen's wives. Their children wear checks. It's why I won't buy Three-M tape. Honey, deck yourself out in tweeds. That camel's hair coat isn't becoming to you. It makes your eyes too pronounced. *That* lets us see the lurching of your thoughts."

A silly thing to think about. But it cheered him up. Nothing had happened to Esther. She'd been in a rush this morning, that was all. Everything would be very sensibly explained.

He looked over the grounds before entering. Esther's car hadn't been touched. Last year's leaves had been raked from the bushes beside the house. Everything else was the same. There were no suspicious rises in the grass, no new burial mounds. He heard music from the upstairs radio as he came in by the back door. The kitchen was tidy, the counters gleaming. A woman was singing a song about a lost love. Roberta Flack, maybe. He heard another voice, much muted, singing along with her.

Esther, when she was happy, often did that. It sounded like Esther. He dropped his case and rushed up the stairs, calling her name. Smiling. Eager to hold her. He heard the splashing of water behind the bathroom door, and rushed in.

Agnes was standing up naked in the tub, panic on her face, reaching for a towel as he charged in. She whirled to regard him, crouching, attempting to cover herself. The towel snagged, twisted at one corner over the rack, and as it snapped loose he saw her feet slide from beneath her. She fell, hard and ugly, before he could even move.

He put his arms under her and lifted her and carried her into his and Esther's bedroom. He lowered her down softly. Her flesh was oiled, warm, scented with lilac. It amazed him that she weighed so little, that she appeared now so frail, so helpless. So goddamned doomed. For she was hurt badly. She'd yet to make a sound; her eyes had not fluttered once.

She looked demure, untouchable, extraordinarily lovely in her pale nakedness.

He pulled the comforter up over her and quickly found extra blankets, remembering that in cases of shock one often became chilled. He knelt beside her, calling her name in whispers, his fingers caressing her cheek, brushing the wet hair away from her throat and shoulders.

She didn't stir.

He reached for the bedside phone and called his doctor.

Ten minutes later the ambulance was there.

"Will she make it?" he asked the attendant.

"Who knows?" the boy said. Then, his mood softening or having done all he could, he said: "She your wife? A dangerous place, those bathtubs."

He rode in his own car behind the ambulance. At the hospital he explained again what had happened. A nurse patted his back and brought him coffee.

He sat in a hard blond-wood chair in the hallway, evaluating his grief, acknowledging his mourning for this person met only a few hours ago. She'd made him breakfast. I *am* home, she'd said. He'd sat with her in his dingy robe and naked feet, secretly studying her. Thinking she was pale, reserved, *odd* — an unlikely member of Esther's circle here in Cherry Vale. Esther was missing. God knows where Esther was, but you had to hope for the best. Esther might show up tonight or tomorrow with a perfectly reasonable — a foolproof — explanation. In the meantime he was here yearning for the life of this stranger, poor Agnes James. *James*. Christ, for all he knew, she was related to him. She had his name. She'd raked the leaves, fed him eggs. She'd washed his robe. It would be interesting to see how that robe came out. It hadn't been cleaned in all the time he had owned it. Partly out of pride, amusement, a certain willful stubbornness. It had the stains of a thousand different mornings, and bore the fruits too of Esther's messy habits, for sometimes, on her lazy days, it was Esther who wore it. Would Agnes James have put it to soak in Zero had she known? He doubted it.

When they let him, he'd go in and draw up a chair beside her bed. He'd hold her hand. He'd sit watching her, waiting for her eyes to flutter, for her first words, for consciousness to come. He'd tell her it was a foolish accident, all his fault. Barging in like that. He'd say he hoped she could forgive him. He'd say too that he hoped one day he'd get to know her better, that he saw experiences of this kind as a conspiracy of sorts, entrapment hatched by he knew not who or what, but that he was grateful for it. For *all* of it, up to the terrible moment when she banged her head. If she hadn't fallen, he would have backed awkwardly from the room, enriched by the shaky vision of her nakedness, and afterward they would have laughed about it. Possibly they then would have gone on to enjoy the dinner she had proposed; together in the kitchen bumping elbows, getting onions chopped, sauces made, vegetables steamed. Dinner by

candlelight in the dining room, a bottle — maybe bottles —
of wine.

— *"Too bad Esther isn't here."*

— *"Yes. Isn't it."*

I never saw you until today, he'd say to her still form on the
hospital bed, but our lives are now intertwined. You've got to
pull through for both our sakes. He'd tell of Joe Ortman's
stories and of the woman on the train in the checkered suit.
That woman would tell you, he'd say, I was being contemptu-
ous of her, with her fat ankles and her age and her zebra purse,
but I tell you contempt is a word gone far afield. I saw her as a
bit of tender bright mercy sent along to enliven my miles. Joe
Ortman's daughter may or may not have a promiscuous edge,
but she's got the right idea. Those maniacs she brings home
only want to carry a little of another life's summons away with
them. You, too, perhaps. God knows why otherwise you'd bear
my name and think to wash our dishes, clean our laundry,
occupy mine and Esther's house. It isn't as though I've never
heard of situations like this: some loony — forgive me, I don't
mean that — escapes from the asylum, thinks to escape from
the street, something goes *poof!* or finally settles in her head,
and she comes in, assured that the house is hers, the husband is
hers, the whole kit and kaboodle is a part of who she is. *"This
is OUR life, Ripley James, mine and yours."* I may have
missed those reports of guys setting fire to swimming pools,
but I've heard of such as this. Christ, I've even thought of
doing it myself. I go to Joe's job for the day, he goes to mine. At
the end of the day we take the train north, instead of south to
Cherry Vale. What the hell.

You drive defensively, God knows, but there you are.

I'm thinking about our situation now. I'm not saying I know
yet what's what, only that certain explanations are not beyond
me. But whatever the situation *is*, I'm on your side. I'm with
you each inch of the way. Esther would be, too. *Will be*, once
she gets here.

I will tell you, too — this speech kept unrolling in his mind, he couldn't stop himself — the doctor doesn't altogether believe me. Some kind of hanky-panky going on, he thinks. He knows Esther, is fond of her, can't help thinking the worst. In the bathtub, no less. He practically said as much. If you had to attack her there, Ripley, you could at least have been careful. The police will likely hit that note as well. You can't blame them. What happens can happen any of a thousand ways. For instance, this morning, if I had come down when Esther called me, rather than keeping my sorry ass in bed, where would you be now? Where would Esther be? Would she be here with us, holding your other hand? Would we be together, waiting for signs of life from you, Agnes James? It could be like that. It could be. Are you listening? What do you think?

He'd give her this speech, some of it.

Yes he would.

Then she'd get well and he — or someone — would take her home, take her wherever it was that people lived.

Dream Lady

IT WAS ONLY YESTERDAY that I was out working in the yard, hoeing out crabgrass, clipping yellow buds for the table, pitching over the compost there where the high hedge hides me away.

"Hot," I said. "Can't take much more of this."

I came inside, mixed a tall glass of lemonade. I drank another, and was standing about, hands down by my side, eyes locked on the floor, thinking about what I might next accomplish outside — or whether it had not already got too dark — when someone knocked at the door.

Knock knock.

"Come in," I said. For the door was not locked and was in fact standing wide open. I have long since given up flying there every time some stranger calls. I've given up wondering whether it's going to be friend or foe.

"Come in," I said. "Come on in. Please come in. We don't stand on ceremony around here. By all means come in, if that's your pleasure."

I heard nothing more. And this aberration, it seemed to me, continued for a good five minutes. Maybe longer. I looked at the stove clock, steadily gnawing at the time, as it is an old clock long past the age when it should be working at all.

"Come on in," I said. "Take a load off. Are you there?"

Light through the window was pale, rather pretty, with that

softness we find out here this time of the year — what my farmer antecedents in the south would have called "dust." Yes, son, it's about dust now, night coming on, about time we put a stop to . . . well, whatever it was we might have been doing.

"I won't bite," I said. "Enter and be greeted. Enter and acknowledge thyself."

Though I believed by now that they wouldn't: that whoever had been there had decided to turn back, or perhaps had not been there at all: that I had imagined that knock at the door.

"All right then," I said, "hold on. I'm coming. On my way. No need to panic."

For by this time I was enjoying the various possibilities. Could be it was someone I wanted to see. Could be it was the daughter I hadn't set eyes on in nineteen years, or her mother, or maybe it was Ma and Pa Rainey in to perform a down-home blues number.

"Yessir, step right in," I said. "Take your boots off. Make your bones comfy."

I talk aloud to myself, you see, more than I should and this was one of these times when I was going at it and glad of it.

"Don't get in a flap," I said. "Speak your mind. Enter or go, stay or depart, never say I'm a person difficult to please or hard to get along with. I'm easy, I'm relaxed. I'm putty in your hands. Do what you please. But if you're still there, then let's hear it. Let's hear it or forever hold your peace."

Good God.

A woman was standing in my hallway, studying the pictures.

"Bless me," I said.

Pretty much up and under my breath, because seeing her there all but knocked my breath out. She carried a thick case, somewhat like an ancient doctor's leather bag, and she didn't yet acknowledge me. Not a flutter my way.

"Lady? Can I assist you?"

Not a nod.

I went back into the kitchen and poured myself another lemonade. Drank it down in one gulp. "Mister," I told myself, "you've got to get hold of yourself. Got to get your wits together. No two ways about it, there's a woman in there."

I came back to the hall. She was still there, still at it, still studying my pictures. Studying my dolls. Nodding hesitantly at one, then going on to another. Up to about the tenth one now, not saying a word.

"Lady?"

Not even hearing me.

So I watched her. I got nineteen of these rascals strung up all alongside one wall like clothes on a clothesline. Big watercolors, not by your Sunday painter either. On the distinguished side, if I say so myself. Real honeys, if a little too melancholy.

She glanced at me and sped up her scrutiny some.

I went back to the kitchen. Forget the lemonade. I got down the jug of real stuff and bolted back about ten mouthfuls.

"Hot daddy!" I said — "been a long time. Whew!"

I turned on a few more lights. Night had gone definitely kerplunk.

"Yes," she said. "Good work. Interesting. I'd say someone in this house knows art."

She had a smooth voice, each word enunciated nicely, like an anchorwoman for whom the evening news holds no surprise. And she was somewhat like that too, smartly groomed, her hair coiffed with an elegant, casual sweep across one side, and with a triangle of deep nudity at her throat that anyone in his right mind would have found alluring.

I found that throat pretty alluring.

She gave me plenty of time to look her over. She gave me a pretty good gaze herself.

"Why are your hands knotted at your sides like that?" she said. "Are you always so tense?"

I tried relaxing a smidgen.

"Lady," I said. "Do we know each other?"

She seemed amused by this.

"Do we?" she said. "What an interesting question! Shall we explore the social and psychological possibilities of that? Do we know each other. What do you think?"

Well, I knew what I thought. I thought I had me somebody escaped from the pea patch, a runaway from the funny farm. I thought I had me a real lollapalooza.

But I looked her over. I wasn't about to get caught by having her tell me she was the cousin I hadn't seen in thirty years or that she was someone I took dancing when I was seventeen. So I looked her up and down, not missing an inch. She let me do it, too. I could tell she even liked it.

"Making any progress?" she said. "Got any inkling?"

She had a nice full figure, no getting around that.

That naked throat, those lean hips and long legs, they were pretty alluring.

"No, lady," I said. "I'm satisfied I never set eyes on you before, not in this life anyhow."

She got a kick out of that. She came through with a splash of pretty high-class laughter.

Then she placed her case down on the carpet and fell serious for a moment, as she stepped forward with extended hand.

"I'm the Dream Lady," she said.

Just like that, without preamble or further explanation, as if those two words summed her up absolutely.

"The Dream Lady?" I said.

Her fingers were soft and warm, her handshake firm as she looked into my eyes with what I took to be an expression of rather bizarre challenge. Bit of the flirt there as well. She was pretty, all right. She was pretty darn exciting. On the playful side, but tall and elegant.

"Yes, I like these dolls," she said — stepping back to peer closely at the signature in the bottom corner — adding, "is the artist a famous person?"

"Oh yeah," I said. "Known far and wide. Bit of a recluse, though. No, you don't hear much out of him."

She picked up her case and peeked her head in through the nearest doorway, saying: "Is this your living room? How nice! May I enter?"

She did not wait for an answer but walked boldly in, scanning the walls, windows, and furniture, and headed for the sofa. She sat on the middle cushion, pulled up her case, crossed her knees, and said:

"You're a very lucky person. I have everything you need. You're going to be very glad I called, yes you are."

She smiled up at me, a longer smile this time, one that held and widened as I stared back at her.

She had me sort of struck dumb. Inside, I had questions going a mile a minute but where it counts in a civil way I had nothing.

Her aggressiveness had me a mite rattled.

"The Dream Lady?" I said. "Did I get that right? You're the Dream Lady?"

"The one and only!" she said. She winked and threw me a raft of different smiles, each one pretty entrancing. She got to swinging that leg: one-two, one-two, a steady rhythm.

Pretty trim, that ankle. Definitely a classy leg. She wore this blue-silk dress, which rippled.

"What kind of dreams?" I said. "Do you keep them in that case?"

I figured she was some kind of cosmetics-type salesperson.

"The normal kind," she said. "Nothing terribly fancy. But they are not in my case, oh my stars no!"

"Excuse me," she said. "Do you mind if I take my hair down?"

Her arms ascended in this swift, graceful motion, and a second later an abundance of hair tumbled down like ink into water.

"I find when the sun goes down I must have it this way," she said. She patted the cushion beside her. "Why don't you come sit over here?"

I grabbed the arms of my chair and remained where I was.

She laughed. It was a nice laugh, but for my money a little too dangerous.

"Perhaps not everything," she said. "Perhaps I don't have everything you need. But enough for a start. Yes, a start, at any rate."

The leg was going at a pretty sharp clip now.

Her gaze was pretty smoldering.

"Everything would be too much to ask," she said. "Yes, *too* much. We can't have that. What would one do if suddenly *all* dreams were answered? How would one *cope*? — is the question. No, no. What we want — all we can handle — is a beginning."

I stood up.

"Excuse me," I said.

As politely as I could I hastened out of the room, turned the corner at the kitchen, and fetched down my jug. I had about ten good chugs. Then two or three more.

"Hot dog!" I said. "Whew!"

Like old times, I thought. Me and this jug.

I had another long pull.

"Whew! That scalds!"

It was then that I felt this strong cold draft on my legs and heard the whistle of wind. Curtains sucked and fluttered and two or three doors slammed shut. The house shook. The overhead lights did a little waltz, and the whole earth seemed to darken a hitch.

It was a regular gale.

The temperature dropped a solid ten degrees in a matter of seconds.

How about that? I thought. Must be a sneak storm come up. Hot ziggidy dog! I thought. Been a long time since I've seen one of these in this neck of the woods.

I got the windows down and the doors secured and reentered the living room intending to ask the lady whether I could get her a nice refreshment — or whether there wasn't someone I could call who would come over and take her away gently.

No one in white coats, mind you. Something dignified.

But the sofa was bare. It didn't look as though anyone had sat on that sofa at any time over the past two decades. Her case wasn't there either. I stepped out into the hall and my nineteen dolls were still hanging. I checked for my wallet and found it still in my back pocket, crushed flat, as usual. I had my garden trowel back there too, so I put that up. I put up the seed packets as well.

So she wasn't a thief.

I checked all the rooms, upstairs and downstairs and even down in the basement, but she was the only item missing.

"Something funny going on here," I said.

I walked outside and circled the house and went out and stood several minutes in my lane, looking both ways. All I saw was the black road and the tree limbs thrashing about and the sky up there looking pretty angry.

Funny way for a dream to behave, I thought.

A kitty came out of the hedge and meowed and I dropped down on my heels and let it lick my fingers.

Ugh, that cat's tongue will make your skin crawl every time.

"Maybe you're a witch," I told it. "Maybe you and that Dream Lady are one and the same. Maybe your broom is over there in my shed and we could both get on it and ride on away from here right this minute. God knows not a soul would miss us."

Thunder clapped and the kitty struck off.

I came back inside and cooked myself up a little dinner. Okra Gumbo a la Nathaniel Burton, the Broussard's man away down yonder in New Orleans, because that sucker knows how to do it. Boil those shrimp shells in your chicken stock, then strain: it makes all the difference.

I sat down and ate it. "What do I want a Dream Lady for," I asked, "when I've got this fine Okra Gumbo?"

"I don't," I said.

"I'm content enough right here by my lonesome."

"Thunderation and bother, that's all another person would be."

"Hold on," I said. "Maybe you've been unfair to that lady. For all you know that lady had only the best intentions. She sure didn't look like no loony."

"Christ, no. Pretty fetching, all in all."

"Good thing she didn't get a chance to open that case," I said. "I might have found myself buying ten or twenty dollars of useless knickknacks. Junky bric-a-brac."

Saltwater taffy, that's what the last one had been selling.

I sat on at the table, staring at my empty plate, hands down at my side, wondering about things. Wondering about my life. Folks would say mine was a pretty empty existence. They'd say I hadn't done much with it.

A recluse, you know.

Almost a damned hermit.

Now and then I kept getting these eerie feelings. Once, the hair stood up on the back of my neck. I kept *hearing* things. A footstep. The creak of a board. Once or twice I could swear I heard water running.

A little "achoo!"

The thought kept swinging in on me that I wasn't alone. That I had ghosts in my attic.

I had a few kicks from the jug, which shook that loose.

I went down to the basement and checked out my bedding plants in their hot-air frames. They were nice and cozy under their glass. Some of those rascals were up already high as my hand, springy and green. The old mushroom crop was chugging along. My cacti table was throwing up blossoms. About a hundred of those shrugged-down honeys, the funniest-looking growths you ever saw, including one that had gone without water for eleven years.

"Makes a guy think," I said. "Boy oh boy."

Afterwards, I tinkered and diddled. "Get your house in order," I said. "If you die tomorrow how would you feel if they came in here and saw you had a leaky faucet."

Water all over the kitchen floor but after an hour or so I had that baby all but stopped.

It was my Fountain of Youth. That leak had been going good and steady for nigh on to twenty years.

Limbs swished against the windows. The sky was black and harumphity but it hadn't yet got down to raining. The zip of lightning now and again.

"Wouldn't want to be a kitty," I said. "Life would be too harrowing."

I went into my back room and worked a while on number twenty. The big one. This was a full-frontal doll close-up on Grumbacher Capri, forty-two by fifty-four, with the doll's face framed from hairline to chin only. Her two eyes, level with mine on the sheet, were like enormous swirly glass buckets. I wanted to get that stare dead-on, to impart to it the unwavering cold innocence of that accusation I'd been living with all these years. To give it the unyielding charge the real doll's eyes held: verdict without mercy, judgment delivered after shock had made cold glass, these two marbles in the real doll's head, the material best able to sum up things.

Yes, daddy, you turd. You sorry mugwump.

You snake.

Such an old doll, my model was. Ragged, bruised, and broken, the pink flesh faded — limp and powerless now except for those piercing eyes.

You bastard.

I wondered if its owner ever missed her. If, of a long melancholy night, my daughter ever said to herself: "I wonder whatever happened to my old doll Ding Dong Belle. I wonder if some other child has her now. I wonder what my daddy ever did with her."

I quit and washed up. I'd never finish her anyhow. She was too damned hard and my hands too shaky, and all the reasons just too worn out.

It was going on to 4:00 A.M. now. The stove clock was clicking and groaning, as if it too was irritated that it had worked all night and got nowhere.

The wind had died down and now hail was pinging against the windows. I opened the front door and watched it awhile, dancing up from the stones and then rolling over dead to ground, like buckets of mothballs that knew they had no future.

"Go to it," I said. "Go at it all night. It's a helluva note for spring, but you're the boss."

I thought about the seeds I'd got in that day and had to laugh at myself.

"Jumped the gun," I said. "Damned if you didn't."

I turned off the lights and climbed the stairs to my bedroom.

"There you are," she said. "I was beginning to wonder."

The Dream Lady. She was stretched out on the bed, against a spangle of pillows, one of my old sketchbooks beside her — raising her arms in an embracing gesture as I stood stock-still in my nakedness, staring at her.

"Come to bed," she said. "I've got it all warm."

She smiled, folding the covers down.

"All nice and cozy," she said. "Climb in."

I thought about it a second or two. A second or two only, then I climbed in.

"I like an early bedtime myself," she said. "You're going to have to quit this night-owl business."

I lay on my back a spell, holding her hand, getting used to her.

"The Dream Lady, you said. That's your business?"

She laughed. "It is hardly a business," she said. "Well, it is certainly nonprofit-making, if that's what you mean. A sideline, you could call it. No, like a great many women I've been bound in by house and stove, husband to feed, growing children, that kind of thing. But that's all over now. Now and then, these days, I get out. I drop in, first at one place and then another. I'm called to it, you see, the way a lawyer is called to the bar or a minister to his church or the way — this is more accurate, I think — a jockey is to horseflesh. Bee to flower? What do you think? Are you interested?"

I was interested all right.

"Good," she said. She rose up on one elbow, leaning against me. Her breasts tickled my skin. Her hair brushed my face and that tickled too. I wouldn't call it precisely a tickle, but something was happening to me all over. I could feel her warmth as though it had got inside me and although my fingers on her backside felt lumpy and gnarled I was coming round to having what I'd say was a pretty keen appreciation of her presence there.

"Good," she said. "I'm not just playing around, you know. You can believe that. I'm your Dream Woman. Your Dream Lady. I really am."

She did a bit of kissing over my shoulders and on my throat and in my ears and around and about my mouth.

"How long are you going to be here?" I said.

"Long enough," she said.

Her legs wrapped over and around. Her voice and her hands — her very being — were beginning to revive something in me. Something, I'd call it magic, was starting to flow. I wondered if I couldn't make a contribution myself.

"That's good," she said. "Keep it up. You're a bit of the old dream yourself."

We were still talking, whispering, researching the matter —

acting upon it — a few hours later when the sun came up.

Much of today as well.

We've been through it all.

She's got me pretty convinced.

Things have got pretty dreamy around here.